KNOCK KNOCK

KNOCK KNOCK
Confessions of a Kiwi Interviewer

TRISH PALMER

upstart press

A catalogue record for this book is available from the National Library of New Zealand.

ISBN 978-1-990003-21-9

An Upstart Press Book
Published in 2021 by Upstart Press Ltd
BDO Tower, Level 6/19 Como Street
Takapuna, Auckland 0622, New Zealand

Text © Trish Palmer 2021
The moral right of the author has been asserted.
Design and format © Upstart Press Ltd 2021

All rights reserved. No part of this publication may be reproduced or transmitted in any form or by any means, electronic or mechanical, including photocopying, recording, or any information storage and retrieval system, without permission in writing from the publisher.

Designed by Nick Turzynski, redinc. book design, www.redinc.co.nz
Printed by Everbest Printing Co. Ltd., China

Contents

1. Welcome to my world 9
2. Children 15
3. Cold calling 25
4. Behind closed doors 29
5. Memorable folk 39
6. Survey methods 45
7. Finding houses 63
8. Access 79
9. Rural remote 85
10. Bureaucracy 93
11. Consents 101
12. Surprises 109
13. Animals 113
14. Weather 121
15. Family strings 123
16. Finding that cross-section 131
17. Connections 135
18. Interviewers 139
19. Other types of surveys 145
20. The human touch 151
21. Away from home 159
22. Outside the norm 163
23. Recognition 175
24. After the survey 179
25. Other interviewers' stories 185
26. The happiest man alive 189
    About the author 191

It's been an exhausting week; you are luxuriating in a rare moment of peace and quiet at home, when there's a knock on the door. Unbelievably, it's someone doing a survey. Really? Now? Your first instinct is to tell me to go away. When I approached your door, I was wondering if this is where I get locked in the kitchen (again), abused (by a parrot), or left holding the baby (literally). Will you be clothed, or stark naked (yes, it happens); all I want is for you to just take part in this interview so that I can stop for lunch, please! Our eyes meet: yours resigned, mine hopeful. Here we go ...

1
Welcome to my world

I have been an interviewer for over 25 years, mostly door knocking or phoning folk to get their opinions on a myriad of local, national or international issues. Everything from how satisfied you are with your water supply and footpaths to measuring a representative sample of the nation's ability to read and do maths. Going into people's homes is an absolute privilege. Hearing your stories has been an amazing, and sometimes challenging, experience. I am visiting you as an observer, but sometimes I come away frustrated that I am unable to help. More often than not, though, you have lightened my day. Every contact has taught me something, not least that we are a diverse and fairly resilient bunch. Also, that most folk are lovely, and that there is no such thing as 'normal'.

Naturally, some encounters stand out, whether it's due to the person, their home, or their circumstances and, occasionally, due to the fear I suffered...

The house looked shut, with old, faded blinds falling apart behind dirty windows, peeling paint on rotting weatherboards, and weed-covered broken paths. Therefore, I was surprised when not only was there an inhabitant but that he agreed to be interviewed, inviting me in. His closed secretive aura did not suggest a welcome of any sort, and he inspected me closely while I introduced myself. His 'come in' was barely an invitation, but I was there to do a job, so in I went.

Stepping into the dark and dingy kitchen, I heard a very distinctive sound behind me; he had locked the door. Terror hit my stomach with such force I thought I was going to vomit. Panic threatened to take over. I was interviewing in a hilly suburb where the residents could see each other, but no one would be looking my way. There was no chance of being heard; the houses were too far apart for noise to travel reliably. The isolation, despite me being able to hear traffic below, was very real.

With huge self-control I stuck to the tricks I'd learned years before. Outwardly pretending nothing was untoward, I sat at the dining chair nearest the door, inviting the man to sit opposite me, and proceeded with the interview. Inside I felt like a mouse, playing catch-me-if-you-can with a very large cat.

As usual, I was wearing sensible flat shoes, and carrying as little equipment as possible, not just for comfort but for safety. Escape is more likely if you can move easily.

The man had a very stand-offish approach to the questions, and he outright refused to answer anything that required an opinion. His answers suggested that he had virtually withdrawn from society. I noticed that there were no photos or pictures anywhere in the room, not even a calendar. A single lightbulb hanging above the sink tried to light the room but failed.

He asked me how I'd chosen him, where I lived, did I have family, and, chillingly, who knew where I was. When respondents ask questions, and many do, I always answer honestly; how can I expect them to take part in the survey if I'm not prepared to be upfront with them? However, my answers vary from being brief and vague through to full detail, depending on the circumstances. Sometimes sharing a wee bit of myself helps establish rapport and trust, which are vital for a worthwhile interview.

Sitting in that locked room, I answered truthfully but kept the details vague, except for one item which I made explicitly clear — the bit about leaving a note for my husband each day outlining precisely where I would be working. This is a safety practice I've always done, so that at least police would know where to start looking if something went wrong. Sitting in that man's kitchen, I was certain that the day had come.

The interview seemed to take forever; I was worried that my fear would show. At intervals I surreptitiously glanced around the room, noting where potential self-defence tools might be found, all the while earnestly being the professional interviewer. I took the opportunity of a supposed coughing fit to turn and take a look at that exit door and lock; thankfully the key was in its place.

With the interview nearing its end, I organised my gear for a quick exit. Still talking, before the man could realise we were done, I was out of that chair, turning the key, and out the door. Fresh air never felt so good!

As I breathed in, a hand touched me on the shoulder, scaring me half to death. I turned, facing the man, who looked at me without threat and quietly said, 'Thank you, no one has visited me for years.' He turned and went inside, locking the door behind him. My heart broke for this lonely man, locked in his silent world. How I wished I'd left something behind so that I had an excuse to knock on his door again.

§

Even in the same street there can be a wide variety of people and experiences. In one middle-class suburb I met someone who had walked through Asia, yet further on there was a resident who had never been out of their own region and had no interest in travelling to explore the other main island of New Zealand.

Every day, interviewing is a voyage of discovery; not only finding valleys, streets and parks that I hadn't known existed, but also meeting ordinary folk who have done, or are doing, extraordinary things, with resilience, courage, kindness and positivity.

There's the neighbour who runs errands for the housebound, the retired couple voluntarily welcoming local kids to their table after school each day to help with homework and make sure that simple needs like clothing and food are met, the lady knitting for charity, the mum caring for her severely handicapped son, the frail gent making his wife a cup of tea, the busy mum coaching her son's soccer team, the dad ignoring his cell phone in order to read his daughter a story, the couple who had put their New Zealand lives on hold to work for Habitat for Humanity in a poor region overseas; the list goes on and on.

Some folk, of course, don't have the resources to help others, yet they too are amazing. For instance, the solo dad trying his very best to give his children a good start in life. He was learning to read so that he could help his kids with homework. How difficult would it have been to front up, admit the gap, and ask for lessons? He was looking forward to being able to read school newsletters, text friends, enjoy community newspapers, and maybe even get his driver's licence, though he didn't think he'd ever be able to afford a car. He was also hoping to be able to read and understand the many official forms that he'd had to sign over the years: tenancy agreements, enrolment forms, custody papers, bank letters. He said he wanted to be a good dad one day. Looking at his healthy, happy, polite kids, it was clear that he already was.

2
Children

Children can be an interesting addition to an interviewer's day. They might ask me to read them a story, dance with them, build Lego, dress dolls, push the swing or join them for lunch. Kids ask questions without reserve: who are you, what do you want, why do you have a badge, are you going to be long because Daddy promised me a swim, do you have children, why is there mud on your shoes, where do you live . . .? Anything goes.

They will also tell you things that Mum and Dad would probably prefer you didn't know. 'I'll get Mum; she and Dad are in the shower.' 'Mum's cross with Dad 'cos he forgot her drink.' 'Dad's got false teeth.'

The interview goes much more smoothly if I take the time to acknowledge the child, thereby relaxing everyone involved. Sometimes World War Three breaks out between siblings during an interview, so the parent needs time to sort it, before the situation evolves into a crime scene.

One afternoon a very excited and proud child insisted I try one of her personally made biscuits, her first ever.

Such a privilege. Fortunately, they were tasty, and my praise was completely genuine.

On another occasion, an intellectually impaired eight-year-old stroked my hair during the entire interview. Her mother was surprised and grateful that I accepted the child's need.

Of course, then there's the child who sits facing me for the whole interview, picking their nose and eating the result; it's hard not to gag, which would be utterly unprofessional and likely to upset the parent. The trickiest situation to negotiate, especially as my instinct is to respond to a child's needs, is the child with the runny nose or who is covered in mud who wants to make physical contact when I'm trying to stay clean and presentable. Usually the parent bails me out, thank goodness.

§

A wee boy of about two insisted that I listen to him count. I crouched down to show him I was paying attention, and away he went; one ... two ... free ... four ... six ... seven ... eight, and then TEN with a triumphant whoop. This is a bit tricky. Some parents expect that I will praise, despite the missed numbers, but occasionally there's one who clearly mistakes me for a teacher and wants me to help the child go over it again to find the missing numbers. Now when a child counts or tells me the alphabet, I find something else to praise, be it their excellent pronunciation or their spacing between each offering. There's usually something that will uphold the child and keep me out of trouble with the parent. And to think I'm just there to interview about something as mild as town infrastructure concerns.

One child sticks in my mind as quite extraordinary. I knocked on the door of a townhouse, completely unaware that the family were refugees who had been in New Zealand for less than a year. A ten-year-old child answered the door, and, as usual in this situation, I asked to speak to an adult. The girl brought her mum to the door, and then translated to the mum what I was there for. I assumed that Mum's lack of English would mean no interview, so I apologised for interrupting them and went to leave. The mum touched my arm, indicating for me to continue with the interview; the daughter translated that the Mum thought it was an important topic and she wanted to have her say, via her daughter.

That wee lass translated every question, listened respectfully to her mother, and then carefully translated back to me. She would ask me what a word meant or for clarification if she didn't quite understand the question, and she reflected the response to me before sharing with her mum. I made sure that they could both see everything I was writing, so that it was open.

I was monumentally impressed. At the end of the interview, the mum indicated that she wanted to ask me a question. She wanted to know where she could find information about hiring a clubroom or hall in order to start up an ethnic dance group for the community. I was able to suggest a few places that may be able to access information on suitable venues, and I wrote them down for her, including how to contact them; she appeared delighted.

Through her daughter she explained that her husband worked all day, and, with the child at school, she had no way of communicating in English during the daytime. However, she had been thrilled to discover that the local city library had a whole section of books in her language, augmented by a computerised request system so she could access what interested her. She said this had been her lifeline.

It's lovely how easily we can connect with folk from different ethnicities if we are open to it. During the interview, in response to the questions, this mum had made some thoughtful suggestions as to how certain public areas in her city could be made safer and more user-friendly. That interview was valuable on so many levels.

§

In a quiet cul-de-sac one morning I inadvertently adopted a wee boy of about three years old. He had been watching me as I made my way around the homes in the street, towards his house. He was riding his trainer-wheeled pushbike up and down the street, doing circles, and racing along the footpath, with no heed of cars coming out of driveways. He called out 'Hi' each time he saw me. It was nearly lunchtime when I finally got to his house. I asked him where Mum or Dad were. 'Mum's asleep with her new boyfriend, and I don't have a dad.' I queried who was looking after him. 'My brother.' I then asked him if he could go and tell his brother that there was a lady at the door. He disappeared inside, coming back with a lad who looked about 13, and who was clearly unhappy at being disturbed. I asked him when would be a good time to call back to see his mum, but he had no idea, as they had been out all night. I suggested, as kindly as I could, that the wee boy was perhaps safer if he stayed inside their gate, but the older boy just shrugged and said he was busy gaming. The wee boy said he wanted breakfast, but the older one said he had to wait until Mum went to the shops because there was nothing in the fridge.

As I moved on to the next house, the wee boy followed, listening from just behind me as I introduced myself and the interview to the homeowner. Upon spying the wee boy, the lady commented that she had only recently moved into the street, but her teenage kids had expressed concern about the lad. They had noticed that he was out most days on his bike unsupervised, to the point that they had not yet actually seen his mother. Confidentiality is an important part of my role, so I could not share with this kindly member of the public what I had seen and heard, even though I was also concerned for the boy. However, the lady said that her teenagers had been giving him fruit and I remarked that it was a lovely thing to do. I also asked her if she knew who to contact if she was concerned; hopefully she understood the implied suggestion.

When I moved on to the next house, that wee lad followed me, despite my encouraging him to go home. At each house he stood just behind me like a shadow, listening intently, and not offering any comment. I was really struck throughout the whole time by his politeness and friendliness. But this child was also hungry and bored, so I fear for his future. What happens as he gets older and starts looking for solutions to his immediate problems? Will this lovely wee lad become a delinquent purely through the need for food and company? Maybe the friendship of kind neighbours will prevent such a tragedy.

Some of the families that I've encountered go to extraordinary lengths to give their kids the best chance possible to have a good start in life. It's not unusual to find parents who run themselves ragged taking kids to after-school and weekend activities, especially sport; the commitment these parents make is awesome.

Even more impressive are the families with virtually no resources who manage to give their kids memorable experiences, just by being creative.

I met a family in a socially challenged housing area who made sure that they attended every free event they could find, even if it meant walking for over an hour each way. They took food and drink from home, so as to keep costs down. This family walked the three kilometres to their local library each Saturday. Despite the nearest bus stop being 20 minutes' walk away, every Sunday they bussed to the beach or a step-off stop to then go on a bush walk or visit a reserve. All shopping, including groceries, involved bussing and then carting the bags home on foot.

This family couldn't afford joining fees for clubs, so there were no sports, music or Scouts, yet the kids were getting a rich childhood with lots of quality parent time — all power to them. This same family had a well-developed vegetable garden for fresh food. The thing I noticed most, however, was that their home was filled with laughter, and genuine, respectful fun.

In another area, I came across a home with masses of laughing children seemingly poking out from every

With more than a little difficulty, I managed to haul myself up without squashing the baby and made my way outside, expecting to see blood and tears. But no; it turned out that the oldest child had picked up a bug and had been chasing the younger child with it, offering to let it eat the sibling! The poor father was earnestly trying to resolve the situation, but those kids weren't really interested as their attention had already wandered to their next game. In the meantime, the baby held its breath, went very red in the face, and made the unmistakable sound of filling its nappy, followed by a stunning smile. I felt so sorry for the dad, who was still getting over the first situation, that I offered to deal with the nappy, but he quite rightly took the baby and did the job himself, very efficiently. Once done, he made a coffee before we could resume the interview!

3
Cold calling

The first phone call, or knock on the door, is always the worst. Will today bring the dreaded dog bite or foul-mouthed abuse? Does someone have a cold or other lurg that I really don't need, or, especially on damp days, whose uneven mossy pathway is going to trip me into a broken ankle?

With phone interviewing, the first contact on a job usually ends in a refusal, as though the respondent senses my nerves and loses faith in the integrity of the call. Then I take a deep breath, talk sternly to my inner self and make the next call, successfully.

When doing phone surveys, working from home can be fraught. I might be halfway through a phone interview and someone knocks on my front door. They know I am home, so assume I will answer, but I cannot; to put on hold a phone respondent who has given me their time would be quite unprofessional. The other side of that is if the respondent has someone come to their door, I always encourage them to answer it. Usually, they put the phone down somewhere and deal with the visitor quite quickly. Sometimes I need to offer to continue the interview at a later time, and we set an appointment.

However, on more than one occasion, the respondent has simply forgotten I was there. During a phone interview, one gent answered his door to a neighbour, and they had a lovely chat; I could hear every word. Once the neighbour had left, the gent then went about tidying up his lounge, humming away to himself happily. I could hear everything, but despite me calling out, he did not come back. In the end I regretfully hung up and then phoned back about an hour later. To save him any embarrassment, I apologised to him, saying that the line had been cut off and could we continue, to which he readily agreed.

§

With door knocking, getting the first interview or appointment under the belt usually resolves the nerves, as most folk are friendly and welcoming. If there is a particularly nasty encounter, taking a couple of minutes to remind myself of the value of the work usually calms things down, but not always.

Of course, some interviews just leave me feeling a bit stunned. One of these was a young woman who was sweet as light with me: all smiles, polite words and thoughtful responses. The whole image was completely spoiled by her response to her kids. They were in the lounge having a whale of a time pillow-fighting, as kids do, with much hilarity.

During the interview, every few minutes the mum

would say to me 'Excuse me a minute,' and then yell at her kids to 'Fuckin-well behave or I'll skin you alive' or 'I'm going to cut your bloody throats if you don't go and clean your rooms.' This went on and on, yet the kids took absolutely no notice. Clearly, it was just plain normal. What I couldn't fathom, apart from the threats, was that she would then turn back to me, all sweetness and light again, as if nothing had happened.

Other folk, however, are so lovely that if we had met under other circumstances, I am sure we could have been friends. They're people who share common interests, or with whom there was an instant rapport, usually cemented by laughter over something. These encounters make it difficult to stay in the professional role, as I'd love to accept the cup of tea offered and put aside the workday to simply enjoy their company. Hopefully, they felt as blessed by the encounter as I did.

Sometimes folk very generously offer little gifts, like fruit from their garden or some biscuits just out of the oven. More than one avid gardener has tried to press seedlings onto me, and occasionally a child offers me a picture they've just drawn. It can be quite tricky to say no without causing offence. One family with four lively kids would not take no for an answer, presenting me with a dozen eggs. The kids were so earnest in their offering that I didn't have the heart to tell them I already had chooks at home. They had parcelled the eggs up and tied them with a bow. During the interview I had become aware that this family was struggling financially, yet they were not only doing everything they could to survive but were healthy and happy. They had a stall at their gate, selling eggs, vegetables and fruit from their garden. It was astonishing what they were producing on their town section, and the kids were highly involved. I accepted the eggs, so as not to offend, but gave some thought as to how to repay them quietly.

A few weeks later I happened to be passing by and dropped some cash into their honesty box at the gate, with no note. The eggs they had given me went into the letterbox of another family I had interviewed who were also struggling, though I took the bow off first!

4
Behind closed doors

When approaching a house or unit, there's always an element of surprise: something that catches your eye. It might be as simple as an unusual flower, a handcrafted door-knocker or a humorous welcome sign. Whatever it is, these little things enhance the interviewer's day. The trick is, of course, to retain the householder's privacy by keeping my thoughts to myself.

Sometimes the surprise is inside; there may be collections of model toys, a craft area set up or some kind of homage to a deceased person. It's amazing what interests people. I've seen a whole room dedicated to things French, even though the person had never been to France. Then there is the house full of salt and pepper shakers or dolls, or newspapers. I've interviewed belly dancers, prostitutes, policemen, hermits. Every door has an interesting story behind it, but it's rare for the interviewer to get more than a glimpse; professionalism means no prying. Stick to the job, then leave.

One house on a hillside had a pair of binoculars on the dining room table, so that the housebound person could watch all the doings in their neighbourhood. He would sit there all day, watching and speculating about his neighbours' activities to his long-suffering wife. I did wonder how those being spied on would respond if they discovered just how closely they were being observed.

Often the outside appearance of a home completely belies the activities within. In a slightly time-warped seaside village, comprised of mostly older, somewhat dilapidated homes, I approached a standard 1960s' three-bedroom box-like home, not surprised by the obligatory concrete path to the door, kitchen window facing the road, tired low stucco fence dividing the road frontage from a patchy lawn, and neglected flower border. What had once been a carport, attached to the long shady side of the house, had been filled in to create an attached shed.

Meeting the couple who lived there, I realised that this home, once their pride and joy, simply showed the same ageing that its lovely owners did. I was warmly invited in.

A deep smell of wood oil assailed my nose as I entered the simply furnished, comfortable lounge. The smell was too thick to be from oiling a piece of furniture; this was all-pervasive, hanging heavily in the air like a cloak. I was curious, but of course couldn't ask.

After completing the interview, the lovely couple asked me if I was a sea person, into fishing or boating. I confessed to a penchant for marine fishing but admitted that I knew little about boats.

The husband was fidgeting so I got up to leave, but he

asked me if I'd like to take a look in his shed. From some folk this would feel threatening, but this man's eyes were pleading, Labrador-like, and, given that I was still curious about that smell, I followed him.

When we stepped into the built-in carport, I couldn't believe my eyes. There were beautifully hand-crafted wooden clinker boats in various stages of construction, from newly shaped planks not yet united into a boat to a carefully stacked stock of completed graceful craft waiting for new homes. There were varying sizes, from the small two-person right up to an eight-person craft. Stunningly beautiful wooden paddles hung along the walls, looking like art forms. The gent showed me how he worked each piece of timber to find its special shape and finish, and how he put them together. Hundreds of hours spent lovingly forming individualised treasures. He didn't advertise his boats, firmly believing that each one would find its rightful home through word of mouth. This work was his retirement; he told me that when he couldn't do it any more his life would be done.

Later, back on the footpath, I looked again at the dilapidated street and the tired stucco home, fully appreciative of the privilege it is to be an interviewer, seeing and learning things in unexpected places.

In another coastal area, a few weeks later, a cold, windy and very wet storm was battering the coastline as I approached a large, modern architecturally designed home nestled on the clifftop. I was taking a hammering, with the storm rearranging my hair into the scarecrow look and water trying to seep into my shoes. My paperwork was fighting to fly away, and I was certainly not presenting the professional appearance that a home of this calibre demanded. The entranceway to the house was quite forbidding, with a tiled entry leading to a very large, firmly shut door. There were no signs of living, or personal touches, to welcome the visitor. Everything about the place shouted closed, rich and minimalist. A security camera was tracking me as I walked up to press the bell.

I was surprised therefore to be warmly invited in, and what a joy that home turned out to be. First, there was the floor. My feet wanted to curl up into the tiles, as the warmth from the under-floor heating was like a hot-water bottle for toes. I was shown to a lounge which appeared to be sitting almost over the sea. With the storm spectacularly thumping at the windows, the waves churning below and the wind picking up sea spray and throwing it about with ferocious intensity, I felt like I was somehow a part of it, yet cosy and warm. It seemed slightly surreal to be sitting in such luxury watching nature vent her might only a few feet away. The chair I sat in had another surprise: it was heated too. My back and bottom were gently warmed as I worked. It was such a lovely experience and restored my settings for the rest of the day.

Conversely, I was working in an area of challenging socio-economic poverty when I interviewed a family who had virtually nothing. The kids slept on shared mattresses in one corner of an uninsulated garage, with Mum and Dad in another. They had a BBQ for cooking, a bucket for washing and dishes and an illegal toilet down the path. The only doorway was the roller-door, so in winter if anyone needed to go in or out, the scant heat was sucked out, leaving everyone cold. This family were renting the garage as they could not find anywhere else to live, despite both parents working. Life was an almighty struggle, yet these folk were smiling. They not only had my empathy at their plight but also my deepest respect; they were trying so hard. It's hard to fathom how it must be for parents to be raising children in situations like this.

Then there's the just plain filthy. I've interviewed in houses that were so dirty that I felt as though I needed to shower afterwards. Rotten food, beer bottles, dog poo, junk and old nappies make for interesting vomit-inducing smells, and any invitation to sit has to be accepted with care. The problem is to make sure that the respondent gets no hint of how I am feeling inside; it's my job to get their opinion, not sit in judgement of how they live.

Interviewers are recorders, gathering data on people's opinions and activity. However, we are also human, and sitting down with another human being often brings connections and raises emotions. Being in situations where folk are struggling with simply living is particularly difficult, especially if I know of resources which could help them. Interviewers cannot suggest solutions, as this type of interference instantly removes impartiality and confidentiality, and it could reflect negatively on the client if the respondent took offence. The only exception to this is if we believe a person to be in some kind of danger, such as from abuse.

Being an observer rather than participant can put the interviewer in unusual situations. I've interviewed a young mum dying of cancer who was puffing on an illegal drug in front of her children, and I've also visited a home where there was a marijuana plant growing in full view in the lounge. The law-abiding part of me had red flags flying at full mast in both cases, but interviewers must abide by the privilege of being trusted as a confidential observer. If we start telling authorities about everything we see, we put ourselves and our families at risk, as well as making those communities more wary, thus potentially skewing survey results.

While the interviewer must be careful to be non-judgemental, there are situations that can create a real dilemma. One afternoon I came across a home in a small town where a young mother was allowing local youth to smoke dope in her garden shed, hidden from view of their families, which left me conflicted. As a parent and law-abiding citizen who has seen the effects of drugs first-hand, I was appalled and every instinct yelled at me to inform someone, but the other side of that was the fact that it would be easy for the woman to work out who had informed, despite the anonymous phone line that police offer. The woman knew my name and would only need to go onto Google to find me, so there was potential for my own family to be put at very real risk. I agonised over this for weeks, and in truth it has never really been resolved in my head or heart.

Interference in a community can be really tempting for interviewers, and I confess that I have succumbed occasionally, in a creative kind of way...

An old man, living in a rural area, lamented to me that he had no one to go fishing with, but he no longer felt safe going out on his own. Fishing was his passion, and he really missed it. At the very next house, two and a half kilometres down the road, a retired gent who had just moved to the area asked me if I knew any keen fishermen as he wanted to learn where the best spots were. This put me in a real dilemma. Confidentiality is critical, yet here were two men who could make a worthwhile connection. In the end I salved my professional and personal conscience by asking if the newcomer had met his neighbours yet. I explained that in rural areas it was perfectly acceptable to simply turn up and introduce yourself, and maybe they would know of someone. By the time the interview was done, the man's wife had whipped up a batch of pikelets, intent on sending her husband 'next door' to meet the neighbour. I really hoped they discussed fishing!

§

Each day, public television news broadcasts bring opinion polls, statistics and survey results into our homes. If the information is too distressing to see or hear, viewers can simply press the mute button. The interviewer who collects that data up close and personal looks into people's faces, hears their pain and observes without resolution.

One afternoon I approached a house in a social housing area, where a lady my age was shifting rubbish from one side of her section to the other. There were tyres, washing machines, old furniture; all items too big for a rubbish bag. She explained that every few months she sorted the growing heap of rubbish to make sure it looked tidy. She had some wooden pallets and was restacking all the stuff onto them. With no car, and no spare cash, she had no means of disposing of these bigger items, but at least sorting it made her feel a bit better. This lady recycled everything she possibly could and had a productive vegetable garden. When she'd moved to the property there had been no recycling bin, even though every property had been allocated one bin years beforehand, when the local council's recycling scheme began. In an effort to obtain a replacement bin, this lady had caught the bus into town to see a council staff member, only to be told that the property owner would need to apply for a replacement bin, which would be supplied at cost. When she explained to the person at the council that the property owner was the council themselves, she met a brick wall; they simply refused to replace the bin, shrugging it off as a matter for the previous tenant. She was offered the chance to purchase a replacement bin, but as a beneficiary she could not afford to buy one. How sadly ironic that the council, as landlord to social housing, would not do what they expected private landlords of less-needy tenants to do.

 In desperation, with recyclable items piling up in her house, one night this woman walked several kilometres to an area she thought of as a wealthy suburb and stole a bin, dragging it all the way back to her place. She felt bad but justified it by assuming that rich people would be able to afford a replacement bin. She admitted that she had been terrified that she might get caught, but she had to get rid of the recycling somehow, and dumping it on the street was not an option for her. Reflecting later, I wondered what I would have done in her situation.

Her explanation opened my eyes to what was happening in her area. Nearly every house had a stack of rubbish somewhere. How can they clear it, realistically? Is there a scheme that can assist? Maybe a skip provided to their street once a year? It's so easy to look from outside, see the rubbish and judge, but interviewing gives a glimpse of the reality for these folks; good people battling against huge odds.

5
Memorable folk

Several years ago, there was a man in the area we were living in at the time who I knew well enough to speak to, and we'd had the odd laugh together. He was married, with kids of similar age to ours, and lived in his own home. He had a full-time job and turned up regularly to watch his kids' weekend sport. At social gatherings he'd have a laugh, engage in conversation and enjoy a beer. He was a fairly ordinary bloke in a middle-class setting.

Come forward a few years, and I knock on the door of a one-bedroom unit in a social housing area and, to my dismay, he opens the door. His lounge is sparsely furnished with mismatched table and chairs, a couch and a TV. There are no photos, pictures or books. He was clearly embarrassed by my presence but agreed to be interviewed. I stuck to the job at hand, which settled him. After the interview he took a moment to tell me what happened to him; out of the blue, mental illness had struck. He had been too ashamed, afraid and proud to admit to a problem or ask anyone for help, as mental ill-health only happened to crazy people, so he turned to alcohol rather than get help; it was easier, private and temporarily made him feel happy and back in control. Sadly, the alcohol and the ill-health deepened, and he lost everything: his job, wife, kids and the will to live.

This man, one of us, had become a shell, lost and afraid. As I walked back to my car, I couldn't help reflecting how fragile our existence can be, and that, but for good fortune, there lies a sadly formidable path.

Under the rules of confidentiality, I am unable to let his old friends know where he is or offer support in any way, but I do sincerely wish him well and hope he finds his way home.

Another man remains memorable for a very different reason. It was to be the last interview of the day. When I'd called earlier in the day, the resident family had all been very busy with weekend gardening being slotted between church-related activities. The middle-aged father had readily agreed to take part in the survey, as long as I could come back at an appointed time, explaining that the family would all be out, so he could concentrate on the topic.

I was mildly surprised when he opened the door dressed only in a bath robe. He apologised, explaining that he was running a few minutes late and had just got out of the shower. I offered to wait while he got sorted, but no, he was keen to proceed, dressed as he was. He led me out to their very private back deck which overlooked a beautifully lush native garden. There was a bellbird in full voice, a pair of tui playing in a tree nearby and fantails darting around us collecting their dinner. Such bush-like settings are usually very relaxing, especially late on a summer's afternoon.

The gent sat opposite me, with his robe barely shut across his chest, and the bottom corners open enough for me to see his knees. Sipping on red wine, he reclined like a Greek god would, as though awaiting maidens to hand-feed him grapes.

Firmly keeping to the job at hand, I began the interview, despite his attempts to divert the conversation. He spoke lazily; he was now totally different to the busy father he'd been earlier in the day.

As the interview proceeded, he 'readjusted' that robe in small increments. Eventually it had been opened so far as to leave practically nothing to my imagination. Experience makes the interviewer well-practised at not outwardly reacting to ridiculous situations; my eyes remained firmly on either the gent's face or my paperwork.

Being outdoors enabled an easy exit. I would not have liked to go through the house where we would have been within arm's length in an enclosed space. The only thing I will say is that the popular assumption of some correlation between feet size (his were big) and certain other body parts is a total myth!

Another man remains memorable for his nervousness about the time the interview was taking. It was nearly lunchtime and his interview was almost done. The respondent, a retired gent, was clearly watching the clock, and as noon approached he asked me more than once if we would be done by 12. The interview was being conducted in his detached workshop, and we were making good progress, so I was confident of meeting his deadline. Wanting to show empathy, I asked him if he had an appointment, but, no, the truth was much more interesting. His wife, whose domain was their house, had very strict rules, and years before, when he had retired from the workforce, she decided that the hot meal of the day would be at 12 o'clock. He had learnt the hard way that if he wasn't there, ready to eat, at five past twelve his meal would slide into the rubbish bin, and the kitchen would be declared closed until his biscuit at afternoon tea — three o'clock on the dot! I made sure that the interview finished at five to twelve.

Another gent, the owner of several businesses, very well-known in his local area, made me feel very welcome, explaining that he understood the need for quality surveys, so he was happy to take part.

Rumour had it that he was a multi-millionaire; his extensive philanthropy certainly suggested that this was the case. He and his wife lived on a relatively modest lifestyle block which exuded a lovely homely feel. They weren't flashy people, but certainly the vehicles and equipment were good quality.

We were sitting out on their sun-filled back veranda, partly protected from the heat by a lush grapevine overhead. The restful view extended out across the lawn, productive vegetable garden, farmyard and paddocks to hills in the distance.

The interview was proceeding normally when this highly rated businessman said, in response to a question, that he could neither read nor write. I smothered my surprise, but he must have assumed it, as he went on to explain.

As a child he had completely failed to recognise numbers, letters and words. They had all been gibberish to him, and still were. However, his parents had encouraged him to find what he was good at, refusing to accept that he was 'dumb'. He developed coping strategies, including being handy enough with verbal language to avoid any serious bullying. He soon worked out that he was extremely good at identifying other people's skills. In addition, he came to recognise that not only was he able to do complex maths in his head when given problems orally, but he also had a highly developed memory bank, and that he could get people to do things.

Leaving school, still unable to read or write, he decided to use his talents to build up a business. He surrounded himself with trustworthy people who had the skills his business would need. As a business strategy, he insisted on daily talkfests and rewarded good work with bonuses, days off and the like, thus ensuring not only good communication but also loyalty from his staff. In that way, he had gone on to own several companies, as well as developing a lifestyle which meets his social, financial and other needs. His message was clear: find your skill, surround yourself with good people and treat everyone well. It worked for him.

6
Survey methods

Busy people sometimes suggest that they be emailed the questionnaire, or that it be left for them to post. They assert, quite rightly, that then they could do the interview at a time that works best for them, and so it will be less invasive.

There are several reasons why this is not a reliable option. First, trials have shown that the response rate is very low, making the survey inaccurate as a representative sample. For busy folk, a survey is rarely going to rise to the top of their priority list.

Generally, people don't like giving out their email address and if they are sent a mass email, their spam blocker will activate, so they don't receive it.

More importantly, on the survey itself, when asked for responses other than multiple choice, folk are most likely to be expedient, saying something like 'good', 'bad', 'okay', which doesn't say why or in what way, thus reducing the quality of the results. A phone or face-to-face interviewer gets the interview done within the timeframe, with a high accuracy rate and quality clarification, all of which makes the study worthwhile. Some online surveys get response rates as low as 3 per cent, which is hardly a representative sample!

Interviewing for quality involves probing. For example, if I ask what the local park is like, most people will say, 'It's good.' Probing involves finding out what good means. The final result may end up looking like 'easy access, child-friendly playground, ample toilets, shaded areas, enough picnic tables, but the slide is a bit damaged', which is a far more useful response for the client to work with.

§

Heading out to start a survey, or preparing to make the first phone call, there is always, for me, a moment when I have to traverse a large mental block wall. No matter how well I know the material, or believe in the value of the particular study, fear threatens to overcome my ability to do the job.

With door knocking it's the fear of the unknown: is today the day I get badly bitten by a dog (it has never happened), or get abused or attacked in some way?

For phone work, it's the fear of rejection, of folk thinking I'm a scammer/sales agent/religious nut, threatening their well-being.

There are tricks to overcoming the fear. With phone work I often get a refusal with my first call. Respondents will pick up on anxiety and therefore not trust the caller. That first refusal usually knocks some sense into me. Then I take a deep breath, and get on with it, confident and friendly. As with all surveys, the industry minimum standard of positive responses from eligible folk is 65 per cent, but I usually achieve in the 85 to 100 per cent range. The better the response rate, the more accurate the results.

Normally phone surveys require that calls are made between 4 p.m. and 8 p.m. weekdays, and 10 a.m. to 8 p.m. weekends. I have an alternative view on appropriate times, so I make my approach differently. My calls on the first day of a phone survey start at 10 a.m. on a weekday; elderly folk are much more likely to agree to a call during what they think of as business hours. Evening calls can unsettle them, and it interrupts their routine.

Phoning that first day also quickly cuts out the disconnected phones, allowing replacements. I never call between 5.30 and 7 p.m., unless it's for an appointment. This is still meal, family and news time in most households, and I like to leave people alone. The same applies to Sunday mornings.

Whether I am phone calling or door knocking, if there was no reply to my first call, the second call always feels comfortable for some reason; maybe because the house entrance is familiar in the case of door knocking, or I've heard the person's answer machine voice in the case of phoning.

When door knocking, if it's obvious that the intended home has visitors, something is going on, or they are just going out or arriving home, I skip the house and return later in the day. There is little point in intruding at inopportune times, which just irritates people.

While my family doesn't celebrate Mother's Day or Father's Day, I don't interview on those days as they are special family time for many folk. Door knocking after dark, unless through an appointment, is strictly forbidden for both respondent and interviewer safety.

Offering to make an appointment, whether I am interviewing face to face or on the phone, puts the respondent in control, and helps get a good outcome; they can choose a time that works for them and then they don't feel harassed.

Of course, some folk use an appointment as a way of avoiding taking part, but tenacity usually pays off. When I do eventually get hold of them, the first thing I do is apologise for missing them, so as to deflect any negative feelings they may have about their own actions.

For phone appointments, calling back five minutes late often works best; human nature means folk are usually running slightly behind, so it relieves the pressure.

Refusals are a natural part of an interviewer's life, usually shrugged off through knowing that the person has lost an opportunity to have their say. When I knock on the door or phone a household, there is only about 10 seconds to convince the person that I'm not a scammer, thief or rapist, and that taking part is worthwhile. I'm also very conscious that I am interrupting their day and that there may be things going on in their lives that have priority. Randomly contacting a household, only to discover that someone there has just died, provides a ghastly moment, which can only be responded to with sympathy and a quick discreet withdrawal.

One lady I called on had just had a call from her family in the UK to say that her twin had died. This lady had no family here and was just bereft. I put aside my work; her needs were bigger than any interview. I stayed with her, at her request, until a friend turned up. To walk out on her, or insist on an interview, would have been callous at the very least.

As an interviewer, normally the idea is to get an interview with as little disruption to the respondent's day as possible, and get out, leaving a good impression; this is professionalism at its best. Most folk are busy and have their day planned already; the knock on the door from a stranger can be quite intrusive and is certainly personal.

However, one lady I visited was just plain lonely, and she begged me to stay a little longer. It was almost lunchtime, so I took an early break and we had a lovely chat. The odd thing was that I genuinely felt that in another time and place we could have been friends. She had a delightful sense of humour and a fairly good handle on world events. Sadly, her living environment and resources restricted her opportunities for socialising, as is true for so many folk I meet, not just in remote areas.

§

Preparation is an important part of coming across as trustworthy, and the resultant confidence contributes hugely to obtaining a successful outcome. Self-assurance, believing in the value of the work, dressing appropriately and being respectful all play a part. People are generally busy, so being very conscious that I am interrupting their day, asking them for their time, is vital. However, I'm also offering them the very real chance to get their voice heard, which is a rare gift. The odds of a non-commercial survey coming to your door are quite small. For instance, with 400 interviews from a city population of 45,000, and assuming a quarter are under 18 and therefore ineligible, the odds of being approached is approximately one in 85.

People often refuse to take part out of fear that their lives will be invaded in some way. Others are so caught up in a momentous period or life-changing event — exams, stress, celebrations, grief, moving house, commitments — that an interview seems impossible. There are lots of perfectly valid reasons for not fitting an interview into their day. In these cases, I just smile and wish them a nice day; anything to leave them feeling good about their decision.

I do try to convince the really busy person to take part, though. If we only interview those people who have plenty of time, the results will be skewed. The busy person is more likely to have experience of whatever the survey topic is, and they will have very valid opinions, so it's essential that the interviewer finds a way to include them. This is usually achieved by being flexible with appointment times. I've interviewed at 10 p.m. or even 6 a.m., as that's the time that worked for the respondents' lifestyle.

One of the strangest refusals I ever had came one sunny morning in an old, established suburb. A young man in his thirties was sitting outside his slightly shabby elderly villa. The house's unkempt air belied its good bones and quality design, somehow reflecting how the young man looked, with his tousled hair and unshaven stubble. He was puffing on a smoke and looked to be enjoying the sun. As I entered the gateway, I called out 'Hello'. He looked up, responded with an echoing 'hello' then stood, dropped his smoke onto the ground, and walked straight past me to the open front door, went inside, slammed the door shut and locked it behind him! I have no idea what he thought or why my friendly 'hello' was so threatening, but I do hope he is okay.

A frustrating refusal is when the person spends 10 minutes telling me that they're too busy to do the interview, then flays me with their opinion on the subject at hand, when we could have completed the interview in the same amount of time.

One of the funniest refusals I have had was from a woman who told me that her mother had just died. The phone was ringing in the background as she spoke. Naturally, I apologised for interrupting her at such a terrible time and prepared to leave. As I was turning away, her husband came to the door to say, 'Hon, your mother is on the phone wanting to know if we would like to go there for tea.'

The woman got all flustered and called me back, clearly embarrassed, apologised and offered to do the interview. I trod carefully, as I didn't want to rub her face in her obvious discomfort. In the end we did the interview sitting outside on her deck. Afterwards she told me that the interview had gone much better than she'd expected, and that I was welcome back anytime.

Some refusals happen before I even get to say hello. I've been threatened, yelled at and had folk say they are calling the police before I've even stepped onto their property. It's sad that people can feel so vulnerable in their own homes. Sometimes it's possible to turn it around, by inviting the person out to join me at the gate. I've been known to walk by later and see a different person outside, approach them and get the interview. That household has the right to have their say, regardless of a single person's initial response. However, I do not go inside a house where I've been threatened or yelled at, as personal safety is paramount.

The only refusal which ever really stuck in my craw, and still does, was from an 18-year-old girl. The home was brand new, in an upper-middle-class seaside town, and the girl was the randomly selected respondent. When she came to the door, I explained what I was there for. She looked me up and down in a lengthy silence, sucking in her cheeks in clear disapproval. Finding me wanting, she said, 'No thank you' with a truly sneering smile. Then she went on to add: 'I know you won't mind because you must get this all the time, but people like me don't need to give people like you any of our time. Bye.' And she shut the door, leaving me gobsmacked. The condescension in her voice really got to me, despite my knowing that I was doing work specifically designed to benefit her community. I had a strong desire to knock on the door again and verbally fight it out, but of course I didn't. I left the property deeply upset and took a few moments to regain my equilibrium before carrying on, interviewing the nicer folk in her neighbourhood.

I trust that life treats her kindly, despite her snobbery; if she ever finds herself consigned to a socio-economic grouping below her perceived personal status, I sincerely hope that she finds the resilience to adapt.

Sometimes the disappointment of not getting an interview can be totally outweighed by a moment which lifts my day. Such was the case when I approached a two-storeyed block house in a family suburb. The sign on the entranceway said 'Haere mai'. There were cars in the driveway, work boots at the door, and the lovely smell of cooking emanated from the open kitchen window. Overpowering all of this was the most wonderful rock music, belting out so loud it seemed to shake the house walls, escaping every open window, blessing the whole neighbourhood. Knocking on the front door seemed futile; the chances of being heard were about nil.

Knowing the piece of music well, I tried to time my knocks for the quieter periods within the song, but to no avail. At the end of the piece, I thought I had a chance but, no, the next piece began almost immediately. After several goes at getting heard, I gave up and moved on. I may have never met the householder, but I thoroughly approve of their excellent taste in music!

§

Respondents often ask how they were selected to be interviewed. It feels pretty personal when someone knocks on your door to ask for your opinions or to query how often you do certain activities. For some respondents, it can be difficult to comprehend that the interviewer is never going to be able to remember your personal details, nor do they desire to.

On a normal day I could end up interviewing 20 people, depending on the methodology, the area and the interview length. There is no way that I'm going to remember anything other than general impressions, unless something truly unusual happens, like the day I interviewed a self-proclaimed witch. She had a broomstick at her back door, a black cat prowling the garden, an incense-filled lounge stuffed with taxidermied animals, witches' hats adorning the walls and, in the corner of her kitchen, a large beautifully round, solid silver-coloured cauldron. I dared not ask what she used it for, though there was no sign of any frogs, thank goodness.

Ethical market research companies bind their interviewers to confidentiality clauses, so I can't even share with my husband what I've heard or seen. There are times when I need to offload, though, usually because a person's circumstances have upset me, and colleagues are good for that.

One woman who I couldn't get out of my mind, and needed to offload about, lived in a very wealthy area, high up on a hill with stunning sea views and backdropped by snow-dusted mountains. There were flash cars in every driveway, and the homes were all architecturally designed masterpieces. It was 10 a.m., and the lady who answered the door was immaculate, with a fine linen suit draping a magazine figure. She welcomed me in, picking up a long-stemmed glass of wine as she led me to where we were going to sit for the interview.

During the first few questions it slowly dawned on me that this lady was tipsy, at 10 o'clock on a Saturday morning. Noticing my realisation, she was initially defensive, making a joke of it, but then became quite bitter. She described herself as the model wife and perfect mother, imprisoned in her much-admired home. Her family were out all day working or engaging in sport, expecting her to mind the fort until they got home, by which time she'd have a meal ready and everything prepared for their evening.

She'd given up all her hobbies, friends and career for her husband and family when she got married over two decades ago, and she didn't have the confidence to re-enter the world. She said it was easier to stay home drinking in the view. With online shopping she didn't even have an excuse to go out.

I wanted to hug this lonely lady, but the 'don't touch' sign was up; all I could do was listen. She had everything, yet nothing: no future, no hope and no joy.

§

To ascertain who needs to be interviewed, individual surveys call for any one of a wide variety of methodologies. It may be that an area fits a certain criterion, such as urban or rural. Usually, once we have a starting point, we will call at every third or fourth or fifth house; this is predetermined so that the interviewer cannot choose. If the chosen house is empty or has no one who fits the criteria for that particular survey, we cannot replace it with a neighbour.

Once we've established that the household meets the criteria, there is always a selection process to ascertain who is to be interviewed. This prevents bias, ensuring that it's not just the friendliest, or the opinionated, being interviewed, so as to get a true cross-section of the community.

Criteria are strictly adhered to. It is frustrating for the poor interviewer when there is a willing candidate right there, but the selection process means coming back for someone who's popped out for an hour. Sometimes the identified respondent is away for the entire survey period, so that household has to be missed, even though there are others living in the house. Even worse is when the selected member won't take part, for whatever reason, yet others in the household are keen. This situation requires a great deal of tact to ensure the willing don't feel rejected and that the household is not left in an uproar through one member being angry with another.

The selection criteria are often quite simple, such as the adult with the next (or last) birthday perhaps. Birthday dates may seem irrelevant to the householder, in terms of who gets to give an opinion, but it ensures that the interviewer is remaining impartial during the selection process.

Sometimes this can lead to funny misunderstandings. I explained to the lady at the door, who was partly deaf, that I wanted to talk to the person in the household who had the next birthday. 'Just a minute,' she said and disappeared. Soon, an elderly gent came to the door. 'What's this about my birthday?' he asked. 'I told them I didn't want a fuss, so bugger off.' It turned out that the next day was his ninetieth, and he'd asked his family to keep it simple, so a stranger turning up at the door and mentioning birthdays had touched a nerve. Once we got the misunderstanding sorted, he was lovely to interview, as long as I promised not to wish him a happy birthday!

Occasionally, there is a household member who tries to insist on being interviewed. At one house, the lady at the door got quite offended when I said that I needed to talk to her 24-year-old son. The survey was about local infrastructure, and she was adamant that as the homeowner she should be the only person eligible for interviewing. I pointed out, as gently as possible, that young people use the roads, parks, sports fields and the like so we need their opinions, but she was having none of it. She said that her son was far too young to have any opinions worth taking notice of, that he would have no idea about what council money should be spent on and, further, that only ratepayers should be allowed to have any say about where their rates went. She added that anyone who didn't have the gumption to own their own home clearly had no budgeting savvy, which, in her mind, reinforced her argument. I never met her son, but I did wonder how he survived with a mother who thought he had no right to an opinion at his age.

Then there's the gatekeeper. I love the challenge they present. They will say things like 'He'll never do an interview', 'You're wasting your time' or my favourite, 'We share all the same opinions so you might as well interview me.' In these situations I stay friendly but firm; the opportunity for involvement is only for the selected respondent. It takes all my skills to bypass the gatekeeper without causing offence in any way, but it's important that the correct respondent gets the opportunity to take part.

Some folk get angry when they are not selected, affronted that I've rejected their opinions, and there are even those who will lie to get selected. In a phone survey about a local body, a gent assured me that he was in the under-45 age group that I was looking for. His voice sounded crackly and elderly, but he was adamant, so we did the interview. Towards the end there was a demographic section, which ensures that we have interviewed a wide cross-section of the community. Of course, having taken 20 minutes to answer all the questions, this gent had completely forgotten about his little untruth, so when I asked him the age-group question he proudly told me that he was 98! I didn't have the heart to tell him that I therefore had to discount his entire interview. He had thoroughly enjoyed answering the questions in the survey, and I was left wondering if he had simply needed his time in the sun, being valued and listened to. Thanking him for his time and great feedback, I wished him well and moved on, pretty sure that I had enhanced his day.

§

It's not unusual for a dominant partner or parent to stay in the room to listen to the interview and offer strong opinions on every question. Sometimes I have to virtually hide my paperwork, as they will position themselves to see if I am recording as they would like me to, regardless of their partner's responses. One elderly woman kept on saying, 'But what would you know?' after her husband responded to any question. This woman berated him with her version of what the answer should be, belittling him every step of the way. That interview was torturous for me; I can only imagine how humiliating and disempowering it must have been for him.

Sadly, when there is a dominant person in the room, the chosen respondent will usually change their answers to fit with the dominant person's opinions, simply to keep the peace. This situation requires a lot of tact. I've been known to flutter my eyelashes and ask the dominant one for a glass of water, just to get them out of the room. In one house I asked the respondent to read the answer options for themselves, then give me the letter beside their chosen answer, so that the dominant person didn't know what was being recorded. I got the impression that the respondent enjoyed the power but was pleased to see that they did agree on some things; it would be counterproductive if they had simply been perverse and answered opposite every time.

In one home, the lady being interviewed appeared to be very meek and mild, while her grumpy husband was pacing the floor and talking over her. Being a keen craftswoman, she had knitting needles in her hands, and she was sitting with her back to her husband. I was startled, then amused, when she began answering verbally as though agreeing with her husband but at the same time pointing to her chosen correct answer with a knitting needle. She even winked at me a couple of times, and I thoroughly enjoyed our little conspiracy.

An obtuse objection to not being interviewed often comes from the mere fact that I *don't* want that particular person's input. The person who opens the door or answers the phone might be all set to refuse to take part, but then when I explain that it's not them that I need to talk to, they get all self-important and take it as a personal rejection. Such is human nature.

On the other hand, folk can be very relieved that they are not selected, yet strangely they can be eager to make an appointment on the selected person's behalf. The tricky bit is when I turn up or phone at the appointed time and the poor respondent doesn't know anything about it, having not been told by the person who committed them. A careful bit of humour, or an apology from me, usually gets us over the hurdle, though there have been a couple of times when the respondent has assured me that they are going to kill the appointment-maker afterwards!

Of course, sometimes folk make appointments in order to avoid doing the interview, when they haven't got the courage to just refuse. Having travelled an hour to get to an appointment, it's disheartening to find no one home, or that the respondent is at soccer practice. However, giving them the benefit of the doubt, I persevere and usually make contact eventually. The fear of the interview, and what it may involve, is much worse than the reality. The truth is that if there's any question the respondent doesn't want to answer, it's perfectly fine to skip it and move on.

On the other hand, almost every day I'll strike a talker. There are two basic types.

First, there's the man who was far too busy to take part but then spent longer than the time the interview would have taken to tell me their opinion on the subject at hand and, worse, everything else that is on his mind, from politics ('They're all idiots you know') to what his wife heard in the shop the other day ('It would make your hair curl'). It can be incredibly difficult to extract myself from these folk. The temptation to insert the survey questions into the conversation, thus getting the interview without them knowing, can be strong, but it would be totally unethical so is completely out of bounds. But I do get frustrated when their ideas or thoughts are unique and could have added depth to the survey results.

The other type of talker insists on answering every question with a long-winded consideration and explanation, so that a 10-minute interview is still going 40 minutes later. Bringing these talkers to a quick response without hurting their feelings or making them feel bulldozed can be tricky. Sometimes it's simply that the respondent is lonely and hasn't been asked their opinion on anything for a long time. Interviewers are not there to fill a social gap, and someone is paying for their time, but my heart goes out to the lonely talker, and I always need to take a deep breath afterwards.

7
Finding houses

This may sound silly, but sometimes it's hard to know what is really a driveway. A rutted clay track in the middle of nowhere, with no gate or property number, could lead to a set of beehives or to a cottage tucked away in the hills.

In town, it's usually more obvious, but not always. One morning I was standing on the footpath, looking at what had once been a concrete driveway. Ragged two-foot-tall weeds sprouted from deep cracks in the surface, reaching out to touch each other as though holding hands for support. There was no worn track and no wheel ruts. Both sides of the driveway were lined with six-foot timber fencing, effectively blocking out any view of the neighbours. The property's letterbox clung desperately to its post, held by the remnants of a sole nail. The letterbox's door spring was fully stretched open and spider webs engulfed both front and back. It just looked neglected and forgotten. The house was hidden from the street by a kink in the old driveway. Clearly, no one had walked up this driveway for some time. However, my job is to knock on the door of every identified dwelling. The rules are clear: visit the house dictated by the methodology, even if it's just to record a vacant dwelling. Absolutely convinced I was wasting my time, I took a deep breath and carefully picked my way through the forest of weeds. They retaliated for the disturbance by attaching seed heads to my clothes.

Around the corner I discovered, to my utter surprise, a neat and tidy 1980s two-bedroom weatherboard house with attached carport. Shiny, unused rubbish bins stood to attention in the carport. There were no gardens, but a neatly mown lawn extended right around the house, which was of a simple box-like style, built to a budget but designed to catch the sun, and offering extensive views to snow-clad mountains, over farmland that lay to the west.

I knocked, puzzled about who could live here and why the unkempt driveway when everything else was so uniformly tidy. Also, I was mystified how they accessed the property, as they clearly didn't use the driveway.

A frail little man answered the door. He appeared to be very old, but I was to learn during the interview that he was less than 70.

The house was sparsely furnished, with 1960s items, neat and very clean. There was no sign of living: no photos, books, papers, pets, music, cushions. A dormant shell. I felt that I had entered a museum's 'retro' exhibition, overlaid in dull browns, with very little colour anywhere.

The man was anaemically pale, which raised concerns about his well-being.

He gave thoughtful and clear answers during the

interview, but when we were done, he wanted to talk. I decided to give him a little more of my time. Putting my work aside, I listened as he told me his story, and it broke my heart.

He had been working in Christchurch full-time, and looking after his elderly mother, when the earthquakes of 2010 and 2011 struck. His life until then had included friends, theatre and regular social contact. His childhood home had been destroyed in the earthquakes, as had his workplace. With no job, no home and a mother terrified of aftershocks, the decision had been made to move north. They both had happy holiday memories of the area they moved to and imagined life would be as it had been while holidaying: relaxing, friendly, warm and safe. They had envisaged gathering a network and settling down to become part of the community. They purchased the two-bedroomed house, with its lovely mountain views, and looked forward to their future in this better place.

His mother died unexpectedly in her sleep just a few days after the move. This poor man was left alone, grieving for the loss of his whole life — job, home and parent — in a town where he knew no one, and with no support. He got by initially, going through the motions, clearing her estate, living off their savings until he qualified for superannuation. He didn't know how to garden or use technology. His budget did not extend to fresh fruit or going out, and he didn't have the confidence to approach anyone. The checkout girls at the supermarket were friendly; he went there nearly every day just so that he could speak to someone.

He'd never met his neighbours because six-foot-high

fences don't allow eye contact, and he wasn't brave enough to knock on the door of busy people.

He watched TV, listened to his wee radio or slept in the sun. He used rubbish bags for waste disposal because the bins were too big and unsuitable for getting down his broken driveway. I asked him how he got out to the street, and he explained that he was less likely to encounter youths in groups if he cut through the paddocks to a more open street, so he felt safer going that way. He got a post office box so that he didn't have to clear his letterbox. This lonely displaced man was an uncounted victim of the earthquakes.

In a cruelly ironic twist, I knew a warm, friendly vegetable grower who lived very near to this man and would willingly help. But one of the hardest things about being an interviewer is that we are observers, bound by confidentiality. To do anything to help this man would be breaching his privacy. Neither the company nor future interviewees would feel able to trust me if I was to interfere in any way.

I did the only thing that I could do: I offered to get in touch with someone for him, but he politely declined, suggesting that my listening had given him the courage to try. I will never know if it did.

Certainly, being an observer of people's lives is not without its challenges, especially when interviewing in contrasting areas of town.

As I approached a garden gate on a November morning, two cream-coloured dogs with poodle-like coats yapped their way towards me, louder than any doorbell would ever be. Their funny little ears bounced in time to their feet, giving a great impression of wind-up toys.

The retired lady of the house invited me in, and the dogs immediately went to their beds, curled up and went to sleep, clearly exhausted from their few minutes' work.

The room was cosy, with books lining large shelves. Wonderful paintings adorned the walls showing scenes of rural workers, and three large La-Z-Boy recliners invited the visitor to sit and stay awhile.

I tried to explain that the interview would take less than five minutes, but this dear lady insisted that she brush her hair first, to be presentable.

Her home, a two-bedroom unit, was tucked at the end of a three-unit driveway, in a cul-de-sac which ended next door in a block of single-bedroom social housing units. This woman, who owned her unit, had a lovely yet simple garden in which brightly coloured flowers intermingled with vegetables and small fruit trees.

The interview went well, and we were quickly done. Then she shared with me a worry she was working through. Her neighbour from over the fence, in one of the social housing units, had a problem, and there seemed to be no solution.

The neighbour had driven to the local mall to get her weekly groceries, parking close to the supermarket entrance. After parking, she had popped across the road to drop off an envelope to another business, then returned to her car to get her shopping bag. In the few minutes it had taken her to deliver the envelope, a parking warden who had seen where she went had put a ticket on the car, as the carpark was only for mall shoppers. The ticket was for $65.

The neighbour survived entirely on a benefit, and that

amount of money was more than just significant; it was a body blow of mammoth proportions. The lady was so distressed she couldn't face grocery shopping, instead driving straight home in tears.

She phoned the parking management company once she had calmed down a bit, explaining what had happened. They responded, in what would normally appear to be a suitable compromise, that if she could produce a receipt showing that she had indeed shopped in the mall that morning, they would waive the fine. Otherwise, no dice.

She tried to explain the distress of the fine, its impact sending her home without shopping, to no avail. The lady paid her fine; it took all her carefully saved Christmas fund so now she had nothing from which to get her grandchildren wee gifts for Christmas, and she was heartbroken.

The neighbour I'd interviewed was trying to find a solution that would not only uphold the lady's already battered self-esteem but also enable her to enjoy the gift of giving to her loved ones. Sadly, no solution had yet appeared, and it looked as though Christmas would be gift-less; this was immeasurably tough for a loving grandmother.

Right after interviewing this woman, fate had me moving to interview in a different area of the same town, in a street of stand-alone large homes set in beautiful gardens. There were boats on trailers, motorhomes and caravans parked beside triple garages. Expansive lawns, smooth as golf courses, were adorned with trampolines and swing sets. Not a vegetable garden in sight.

Approaching the nominated house, I was struck by the sheer contrast to the previous area. The doorbell rang a sweet tune and the home's heavy wooden entrance door swung open to reveal a grand entrance foyer in which stood a busy, fit-looking mum and her 12-year-old son. It was almost lunchtime, yet the lad was dressed in a plush dressing gown. The mum answered the questions in the interview pleasantly and efficiently, occasionally asking the son his thoughts. He was polite and friendly, and I was temporarily impressed.

Then we came to a question about what the town needed. The mum responded that the town needed some decent clothing stores. I was surprised as I thought the area was well-supplied, with all the usual big-box stores and large clothing retailers. This pair went on to tell me that the 12-year-old lad only wears label clothing, so they have to shop online for his clothes or fly to Auckland to spend a day accessing stores unavailable locally. He refuses to wear anything purchased locally, even socks!

Standing at the door, listening to this pair earnestly relating how the local town couldn't supply decent clothes, I wanted to scream. The sheer snobbery of the boy's lifestyle took my breath away. I'd just come from an area where a $65 parking ticket had been a body blow, and now I was faced with a child that wouldn't wear anything that wasn't a label. The contrast threatened to overwhelm me; I wanted to drag that lad into the real world, tell his mother she was a fool, and suggest that the food bank could do with 90 per cent of his clothing budget. Of course, I didn't say anything, just smiled, listened and recorded but felt sickened that by saying nothing I was somehow endorsing their extravagance.

Rationalising it later, I accept their right to spend their money in whatever way they like. Being rich, having choice, is no crime, and they are blessed with good fortune.

In the case of the beneficiary, however, I feel frustration that the very fact of her poverty made her so vulnerable. If the rich mum had parked at the mall as the beneficiary had, then popped across the road to deliver an envelope, she would also have received a ticket, so this appears to be fair and equal.

However, it's what happens next which keeps the poor down and the rich intact. The rich lady would probably have been irritated by the ticket, but not distressed, so would have continued shopping, thereby obtaining the receipt which would prove that she had indeed shopped at the mall. Therefore the $65 ticket would have been waived. Where is the equality or fairness in that?

Coming across situations like this has definitely changed my thinking. Where I used to see issues in black and white, hearing people's stories has made me realise that everything is grey. What appears to be a straightforward solution to an issue to one person can be quite threatening to another.

For example, an urban area had no street lighting, so some local folk lobbied for lights to be installed to make the area safer for night walkers. On the face of it, this seems perfectly sensible. Soon after the lights were installed, I happened to interview an elderly lady who lived on her own in a one-bedroom unit situated in such a way that her bedroom was almost adjacent to the street's footpath. For decades she had enjoyed peaceful, calm nights, but since the installation of the lights she was permanently exhausted from interrupted sleep, as well as being severely stressed by fear. Foot traffic had increased significantly, passing right by her bedroom window, and folk using the footpath at all times of the night regularly startled her from her sleep, often with their rough talking and swearing. Once awake she struggled to go back to sleep, huddled under her blankets. She dared not turn on a light, afraid it would draw attention, so she lay there, alone and frightened, listening to the behaviour of strangers just metres away. Loud drink-affected groups staggering home on Friday and Saturday nights not only wakened her but they used the side of her house to pee on. Couples cuddled up against her house wall, not caring whose property it was. She regularly found broken glass and other rubbish outside her home in the mornings. None of these problems had occurred before the lighting was installed, and she just knew that one day something terrible, like a bottle through her bedroom window, was going to happen.

It's the little things that can change lives.

§

One of the great values of interviewing people is hearing their ideas. A man was telling me that he gets lost in his home town, despite having lived there all his life. With advanced age has come moments of confusion, and unfortunately the rapid growth and development of his local area has exacerbated the issue. He loves walking, and his wife is not always available to accompany him. He completely rejects the idea of a minder or walking group as they walk too slowly for this fit, active gent.

However, when he's walking, simple geographic features like cul-de-sacs can cause confusion, so that he loses track of where he is. Street signs usually only display the name of the side street, with nothing to indicate the road or street they are running off. Usually, street signs are on the opposite side of the road, designed to meet the needs of drivers, not walkers, meaning he has to cross over the road to get close enough to read the sign. Unfortunately, by the time he's got there and read it, he's forgotten which way he had been going. GPS technology would help, if only he could remember how to use the cell phone!

This thoughtful man's solution is simple: every urban intersection needs the name of the streets involved painted on the curb or footpath. In this way, walkers and bikers would know where they are, thus empowering them. He pointed out that this would also help in emergency reporting, as often the passer-by informer of a car accident or fire is not familiar with street names. He asserted that folk regularly travel routes where they don't know the individual street or road names. With an ageing population, and the increasing number of elderly folk living independently, this simple measure could add to their security and confidence.

He had suggested the idea to his local council but was told that since the local group who represent the area's elderly hadn't raised it as an issue, it was unlikely to be actioned, which disheartened him. He wants to keep being active but said that the fear of becoming lost, and therefore vulnerable, was beginning to impact on his confidence. Sadly, he was in danger of becoming too afraid to venture out.

Sometimes encounters can be challenging for other reasons. As interviewers we cannot interfere with people's thinking. The bigoted, racist and sexist are all entitled to their opinions, regardless of how distasteful they seem. Maintaining a warm, friendly, professional demeanour is essential when an elderly man says that it's nice that my husband lets me work, or when a respondent says, 'I'm not racist but ...' People's beliefs are formed through their experiences, and listening to people's stories raises the question: if that had happened to me, would I think and feel like that too?

Of course, some beliefs are not based on bad stuff but on simply being different. At one stage I was involved in a longitudinal study which involved returning to the same folk year on year to see how their attitudes and behaviour had changed, or not, in regard to certain topics. Generally, folk welcomed me back, feeling valued by their ongoing involvement. However, there was one household which always gave me pause for thought before I headed their way. Not long after the respondent had become part of the study, they had moved house to a nudist colony! The first time I visited, in my ignorance I was nervous of causing offence by being fully clothed, or by appearing to stare, but of course it turned out to be fine. Having said that, my nerves never really disappeared, as I was way out of my comfort zone.

Sometimes there are things I see that are difficult to comprehend, like the man burning his household plastic waste and spreading the ash on his garden, or the person cleaning out their fridge, throwing away an unbelievable quantity of vegetables just because they were two days old. These kinds of incidents are less common, though, balanced by the truly wonderful people or communities whose actions and care far outweigh the negative. There are so many memorable examples of this compassion . . . an Asian man gently played the guitar to his baby son in the background while I interviewed his wife; a street where the neighbours share their fresh produce and ideas; a woman spoon-feeding her bedridden husband while she was talking to me; a man fixing his granddaughter's car; a lady busily knitting for the local hospital's premature babies; a refugee making soup for her sick neighbour; a couple exhausted from planting trees at a local reserve.

Grandparents proudly show me a photo of their grandchild's sporting achievement; a housebound man makes daily phone calls to check in on other housebound folk for St John; the list goes on. There are so many generous lovely people out there, and it's a real privilege to meet them.

Occasionally, I come across an old school friend or someone I knew years ago, which can be a lovely surprise. I don't interview friends or relatives, though, as it's generally a waste of time and could potentially skew the results as they will give answers that conform to how they view our relationship, saying what they think I expect to hear, thus making the interview worthless.

However, being a stranger can bring about its own interesting challenges.

I had noticed the two men about an hour earlier,

watching me as I worked my way along their street. There was something about their manner which made me uneasy; even Neighbourhood Watch folk are not as overt as these two were being. The street had a cul-de-sac running off it, which I went into, relieved to be out of the men's direct view. I completed a couple of interviews, of about half an hour each, so naturally assumed that the two men would have got bored and moved on. I was dismayed therefore to find them still apparently waiting for me. Their silent watching felt creepy and very threatening. I went back to my car, shifting it closer to where I was working, so as to have an escape plan if needed.

Crossing the street in an effort to avoid any confrontation, my fear became live when they crossed the street too. Then they stood silently, watching and waiting.

Another interview, and then I had to go past them. By this time, I reckoned they'd been watching me for over an hour and a half. Remaining outwardly warm and friendly but terrified inside, I stepped onto the grass berm to go round them, but the younger of the father-son duo stepped in front of me, arms folded, glaring. At that moment two things occurred to me. The first, that interviewing is a mug's game and, second, that I should have asked the person I had just interviewed to keep an eye on me for a few minutes. Of course, I hadn't done that, probably in some ridiculous belief that I was making a fuss over nothing.

'What are you doing in our street?' the son demanded. The sheer aggression in his stance and voice was unmistakable.

'Looking for places with stuff to nick,' egged his father.

Apart from these two, the street was deserted. Not only had the traffic disappeared, but it was as though even the birdlife was holding its breath. No one was going to get me out of this.

Keeping my outward manner unconcerned and warm, belying the churning in my stomach, I introduced myself, and explained what I was doing, including drawing attention to my photo ID badge with its 0800 number. I invited them to give the number a call to check me out, but, of course, they didn't do cell phones.

'What's the survey about then?' demanded the son, with no less aggression.

Upon hearing the answer, the father launched into a torrent of abuse about bureaucrats and the topic at hand.

The son then challenged me to interview him. Checking that he qualified, by getting the household's details, felt like playing with crocodile teeth — get it wrong and die.

Thankfully, the son did qualify, and we did the interview right there and then. Their aggressive attitude didn't change at all, so during the interview I made plans for how I could achieve a quick exit when the interview would be over. Multitasking is an essential skill at times.

Quietly, over several long minutes, I manoeuvred so that I was on the outside of them both. I made sure that they didn't realise that the interview was finishing until I simultaneously thanked them and stepped away. The urge to run was very strong, but I managed to walk purposefully towards the next house. The last thing I heard, said by the son, was the outstanding line: 'And don't come round here bothering people like us again; bloody nosy surveys.' I didn't know whether to laugh or cry, given that they'd virtually forced me into interviewing them.

Deep breath, shoulders back, smile, and knock on the next door where, thankfully, the friendly residents were home.

§

Sometimes there are some very interesting and funny incidents which the interviewer has the glorious opportunity to observe, without getting involved.

A four-wheel-drive vehicle and its attached caravan were backing out of a driveway, with the driver's 30-something wife giving directions from the other side of the fairly wide road.

It wasn't going well. The caravan would back onto the road okay, but then, no matter which way the driver turned the wheel, he couldn't get that caravan to go where he wanted. Tensions were mounting, so I decided to move further down the street and come back later. If a driver is not used to backing a trailer or caravan, it can be quite confusing, and these young folk certainly didn't need me, a stranger, adding to their stress.

After half an hour, with two interviews completed, I was back, but the caravan was in the same place, and the couple had upped their stress levels several notches. A neighbour had joined them, offering useful advice, but still the vehicle and caravan were going back and forth without success, jack-knifing at regular intervals as the caravan turned too sharply for the driver to keep up.

There was a double-width driveway directly opposite theirs, so I couldn't understand why they didn't just back straight across the road, into the double-width drive so that they could just drive forward out onto the road in the direction they wanted to go.

The language emanating from the driver and his wife was getting pretty raw, so I was reluctant to approach. Instead, I went to my car and did some paperwork, though I was still able to see how they were doing, which wasn't well.

Eventually, they went to plan B, disconnecting the caravan from the vehicle and, with much heaving, the three people pushed the caravan out onto the road, then up onto the wide driveway opposite. Hallelujah! Now all they needed to do was reconnect and drive away.

My relief on their behalf soon turned to utter astonishment, and then laughter, as the three of them continued pushing that little single-berth nine-foot caravan back, all the way down the wide driveway to a spot beside the house at the far end. I had thought that they had been trying to back out onto the road, in order to then drive away, but the whole time they'd actually been trying to just go straight back across the road! Oh well.

8
Access

Fortunately, I have a choice of car to use: a large four-wheel-drive or a smaller town car. Which one I choose depends on where the work is that day. For back-country or rural areas, the four-wheel-drive is more sensible, not just for its off-road abilities but also for visibility. In urban areas the smaller car is generally better, especially for finding parking space.

When creating new hillside subdivisions on the outskirts of a city, developers create spider-webbed accessways up steep hills, in order to get in as many building sites as possible, while ensuring every home retains a worthwhile view. In one new area, I noted the dozen or so identical letterboxes all lined up at the entrance to the street I was going into. Householders often like to retain individuality, so, despite the uniformity of the actual letterboxes, each homeowner had personalised their box for identification purposes. There were numbers and in some cases names in gold, silver, red, black, green, using varying heights and fonts. Some names and numbers were lined up level, and there were a couple that were on an angle, but the one that made me smile had attached all their details upside down.

The street sign was standard and did not display a 'no exit' warning, so I was confident that the street came out somewhere, despite it being narrow and winding. The steepness of the street was accentuated by a deep gorge falling away on one side. My town car was in first gear to make the climb, so I was quietly lamenting the decision to leave the four-wheel-drive at home that day. Crawling around a corner, I was aghast to find that the street simply stopped at a locked gate, with a 'no entry' sign advising that the area was a development zone.

To my left was the gorge drop-off, and to my right a lovely brand-new home where someone had unloaded garden mulch on the driveway, blocking the only obvious turning spot. I didn't fancy retreating backwards; reversing down that steep street around blind corners had no appeal, so that just left trying to turn around. Is it better to turn so as to be facing the drop-off, but backing into someone's new mulch, or go the other way, trusting that I'll feel the kerb before inadvertently driving backwards over the cliff? I chose to face the drop-off. Thank goodness for the smaller car! Even then, despite the car's size, it was no simple three-point turn. That street was so narrow that my car's length barely fitted when sideways across the road, so I was forced to inch back and forth, very aware of what could happen if my foot slipped on the accelerator.

Heartily relieved when done, and parking facing downhill, I knocked on the door of the top house and was warmly greeted. Apparently, I'd earned my stripes by completing the turning manoeuvre; they'd been watching and wondering what I was going to do as they hadn't thought that turning was a feasible option. It's the oddest things which can convince folk that you're genuine.

The four-wheel-drive, on the other hand, is very useful in rural areas. I've needed to cross rivers, traverse long rocky accessways that could barely be called driveways and bulldoze my way up muddy unformed tracks to get to homes.

One of the worst was an accessway through a forest, where the mud was over a foot deep, with invisible sinkholes; it felt like a mud-plug track from the four-wheel-drive club competition days rather than a driveway, and it required a great deal of time and skill to traverse. At the top, when I finally got to the house, I was astonished to find a young mum with her newborn baby. Less surprising was that the midwife didn't do home visits to her and visitors were rare.

Sometimes remote coastal areas have clusters of homes and baches nestled around seaside inlets, sheltering from the Pacific Ocean's strength, yet retaining sea views and ready access to fishing and the like. Rooftops, barely visible in the bush high up on the surrounding hills, are often only distinguishable by the change of colour and texture from the trees around them. Noting letterboxes usually helps to work out how to access those homes and how many are up each driveway, but getting there can be tricky.

One lovely spring morning I headed up a sealed driveway, passing three letterboxes at the bottom. I was walking, since I could see that the first house was not far; I'm reluctant to take up homeowners' parking spaces on hillsides if it's not necessary. At that first house I was warned to drive to the second, as it was quite a way up, and that I shouldn't bother even trying to get to the third. Local knowledge is always useful, so I took notice of the warning, but I had to balance this with the need to get a good coverage of the area to achieve a true reflection of the locals' opinions. Thanking the person, I went back and got my car. The drive to the second house was indeed quite a climb, about a kilometre up a bush-clad hill, and I was pleased not to have walked. As with so many of these more remote places, the resident ran her own business from home, and she proudly showed the creations she handcrafted.

When the interview was completed, this friendly artist suggested I think hard before heading further up the hill to the third property. She explained that it was around 2 kilometres of rough hill, with many corners too tight for anything less than three-point turns. She said that coming back down could be terrifying in an automatic car, requiring reverse hill starts and hard braking on gravel. My four-wheel-drive is manual, and I was confident of my hill starts, so off I went.

That lady wasn't kidding! The drive was very tight, with trees blocking any vehicle space on the sides, and steep drop-offs discouraging use of the edges of the road too much. The whole drive required great concentration. I dreaded meeting another vehicle, as there was nowhere to go, and no relief. It seemed to take hours to get up there.

When I finally reached the parking site at the top, the homeowner was so impressed about my having made it that he agreed to do the interview before he even knew what the topic was. He was building his own home, and he said that even the building inspectors were very reluctant to visit, preferring him to email photographs instead. He had no plans to improve the driveway as its challenges guaranteed privacy, and I couldn't blame him. He had native bush coming right up to his door, spectacular views over the coast and out to sea, native birds coming into the site and the most amazing birdsong backgrounding his day.

Sometimes access to homes is just as difficult in the middle of town. High fences, electronic gates, gated communities and hedges can make getting to individual homes quite challenging.

Folk have asked me if I'm invading residents' obvious desire for privacy when I enter those heavily protected properties, but surely every household has a right to express their opinion and have their say about what happens in their community or comment on proposed legislation, as much as anyone else does? It's my job to offer that opportunity. It is definitely not my decision as to who can take part.

Generally, most survey companies don't go into caravan parks and marinas or interview homeless people, but I wonder if that's justifiable, given that these folk will undoubtedly have their own perspective, which would surely augment the survey results in a useful way. With so many folk living in mobile housing, or boats, I believe survey companies should be widening their catchment criteria when doing local body or government work.

9
Rural remote

Working in remote areas, driving vast distances between each house, can bring surprises and special problems. Usually, the worst part is the lack of public toilets; a whole day without spotting a toilet is common, and testing!

In one area, at the second house I approached, I was surprised to be greeted by name, and invited in; the person clearly knew what I was there for. It turned out that the previous person I'd interviewed had phoned them to let them know I was coming, and that the interview was fine. In these more remote areas, we generally visit every house as the draw sample is so small. As I worked my way through the area, I was told who was away, what time Fred/George/Harry next door normally came in for smoko, and often, when I knocked, they were expecting me. It was rural Neighbourhood Watch at its warm, friendly and helpful best.

Sometimes, knocking on the door, whether rural or urban, elicits a 'Come in' from inside, without the person coming to the door. It may be that they are expecting a friend, that they are engrossed in a creation they don't want to move away from, or that they are housebound. I call out a greeting, stating who I am, which usually clarifies matters, but there have been times when the voice has insisted that I come in, to my discomfort. Walking into someone's home without their having met me first feels like I'm invading their personal space. Generally, the person is incapacitated in some way, so this is their usual (and very trusting) practice. One gent wisely had a camera link to his door to provide at least some measure of security and so reduce his vulnerability.

§

A hot afternoon on a dusty gravel road, miles from anywhere, I happened across a set of very old yards where the farmer was working with some sheep. He looked to have been sorting them, as the ewes and lambs were separated, and he was standing at a gate as I drew up.

'Thank God,' he said as I alighted from my car. 'Come and hold this.'

Now, I was looking for the landowner to interview, but if I was to get any kind of rapport with this man it was clear that I would need to help him first. I climbed through the fence and went around to him. The problem was clear: the gate slide had broken, and there was nothing to prevent the sheep from pushing the gate open and escaping. I took hold of the gate, assuming that the farmer would grab something from his ute that was parked nearby.

However, to my utter consternation he hopped into his ute and drove off up the road towards the farmhouse in the distance! I was trapped; if I let go, the sheep would get out and there'd definitely be no interview, but how long was he going to leave me standing there? I waited, and waited, becoming increasingly convinced that I was being subjected to some kind of practical joke. I could just imagine him and his wife having a cup of tea in their kitchen and watching me through binoculars, delighting in my predicament! Still I waited.

After what seemed like an eternity, I was relieved to see the dust of his vehicle as he headed back. Once he had put a wire tie on the gate, and thanked me, he asked me what I wanted.

I did my spiel about the survey, convinced that he would feel obliged to participate. I was sadly mistaken. 'I don't live here,' he said. 'I just lease the land. You'll need to go up to the house to talk to the people that live here ... But they're out for the day.' Oh, well. My worksheet showed an hour's 'break'; I didn't think it would be kosher for the company to pay me to stand in a paddock holding a gate shut.

§

Sometimes it's best to walk or drive away before even making your presence known. Such was the case one afternoon in a reasonably remote area about three hours from my home. I had driven along a farm track to a house that was sitting in the middle of a paddock. The house looked to be maybe 15 years old, but there was no sign of any plants, gardens or landscaping. The drive ended abruptly at the edge of the veranda, so no path was necessary. The house was a bit weary-looking, but the grass, which couldn't really be called lawn, was mown and the place was tidy, with no outdoor furniture or junk to be seen. The house clearly had views across the paddocks and out to sea.

A house plonked in a paddock is common where a dairy farm needs a worker's house, as the milkers usually only stayed for a year or two before moving to their next step on the career ladder, so the owners have no interest in spending time or money developing gardens and the like.

At this house, there were no dogs in the kennel and no sign of life coming from indoors. I heard a commotion away down the paddock and turned to look. A man was waving his arms wildly, running at some cattle, while his dogs were having a party all of their own. One cow had rebelled and headed away from the mob. It appeared that the man was trying to shift the cattle into another paddock, and they weren't having a bar of it. The day was hot, despite a strong sea breeze. As the man ran towards the mob, they all panicked, split into two groups and ran past him, reuniting behind. The rebel animal joined them, and then they all stood looking at the man.

Round 2, though it could have been round 10 for all I knew, began with the man calling the dogs, then walking around to the back of the mob. He sent one dog out on each side of him, in textbook manner, and together the three started to push the mob towards the gate. This was going well.

Just past the halfway mark, the mob slowed to a stop, heads high on alert. One or two milled briefly, before one (possibly the same rebel from before) turned and ran back the wrong way. The man tried to step in its way, hoping to make that rogue animal turn, while blessing it with words definitely not suitable for polite company. This had the interesting effect of encouraging the others to join their mate. That poor man; even from a distance I could tell that he was apoplectic with rage. He picked up some stones and hurled them at the cattle; not a single one met its target. More interesting words carried across the airwaves to my delicate ears.

It was at this point that I decided to quietly withdraw; there was no point approaching him for an interview just then. This was probably a good decision, as when I went past again a couple of hours later, there was no sign of the man, but the cattle were happily grazing in their original paddock, with the gate open to the new block. Presumably, at some point they would have got curious or hungry enough to wander on through; I just hope the man got there to shut the gate behind them.

Going to outlying areas means interviewing at properties known as stations, which are much bigger than the ordinary farm, often covering thousands of hectares. Even their 'driveways' can be several kilometres long, often through stunning farmland and native bush areas. On this day, the only sign of habitation had been the very large letterbox at the farm gate, about 20 minutes previously. Coming over the brow of a small hill, my heart sank. There, below me, were the unmistakable signs of shearing time. This is when all hands are on deck, and no one ever has time to stop for anything other than a drink or food. The last thing they would be interested in would be an interview. In fact, there was a high chance that they would just see me as a nuisance, as invasive as an insurance salesman.

 The only place to turn around was in the yard, so there was no way that I could beat a hasty retreat without being spotted. In forlorn hope I called at the house but, as expected, there was no one there. I went over to the shearing shed, thankful for sensible walking shoes. The sweet smells of sheep, newly shorn wool, sweat from hard-working shearers and rousies, and a coffee urn all assailed my nose, while the noise inside the woolshed was deafening. Not only were the shearing blades humming, sheep bleating en masse, and the clatter of sheep feet on the floorboards competing with the noises of humans working fast, but a radio was blaring in the corner with heaven-knows-what kind of music; certainly, I could not distinguish any song as recognisable. A lass approached me, and I asked for the boss. He was shearing. I made my way over to him, careful not to get in anyone's way, and then stood waiting. Actually, I could have watched all day; I've spent hours in shearing sheds, and have always loved the hum and the smells, along with the camaraderie, though it's not the romantic vision that poets portray but a place of hard work and terrific skill.

 The boss eventually acknowledged my presence by glancing my way and yelling 'Yes?' His hands didn't even pause in their work. There was no way that I was going to ask for his attention, so I simply said, 'I need to catch up with you sometime. When would suit?'

 'Tomorrow, lunchtime,' he responded.

 'Right, see you then,' I agreed and left quickly and

quietly. The next day I rocked up at 12.30 (lunch on a farm is rarely at midday, despite the best of intentions, and I didn't want him to feel imposed on or rushed). I introduced myself, told him what I was there for and got the interview. Flexibility and empathy breeds success in this work, and it's so important that we leave a good impression. Bad news travels fast, but a good experience lays the path for future interviewers.

10
Bureaucracy

Annually, most local authorities conduct residents' surveys, to obtain feedback on a wide range of issues: anything from infrastructure to planning, freedom campers to Christmas events. Listening to residents across the country reveals that most councils generally grapple with similar issues.

Many respondents will talk about issues they have, but also comment that they haven't liked to bother those busy folk at the council about it, even when the problem involves a seriously dangerous situation. One gentleman told me about how he keeps a very long pole especially for when the area floods. He manoeuvres this heavy and unwieldy pole carefully in order to clear debris from the council-owned stormwater drain on his property when the drain overflows, despite often having to be ankle-deep in the fast-moving flood water, in the rain; this man does all this while confined to a wheelchair.

Other folk don't contact councils, out of fear. A lady

on superannuation told me about a tree on the berm outside her home. She was terrified of it, as it dropped branches in high winds, meaning she couldn't go outside on windy days. She hadn't contacted council about her concerns as she was afraid that they would bill her for the work, which she couldn't afford. It was council staff who had planted the tree.

A lovely elderly gent told me that he used a mobility scooter for getting around, but to visit his local shops, which were just a block away to the right of his home, he went out his drive, turned left, travelled to the next intersection, crossed his street, then came back on the other side of the road past his place. When he arrived opposite the shops, he used the pedestrian crossing to access the shops which were on the same side of the street as his home. I asked him why he didn't turn right out his driveway, to go the direct route to the shops. He explained that there was a side street to navigate between his home and the shops, and the intersection slope from the footpath to the road was cambered incorrectly, so his scooter would ground out, leaving him cast and in the way of any traffic. This left him reliant on a helpful, strong passer-by noticing his predicament and lifting both him and the scooter out. He didn't like the vulnerability of being dependent on others to stay safe. He hadn't contacted the council because he had found another route, and he didn't want to bother them.

Another lady told me that her recycling wheelie bin, which council had so kindly delivered, sat empty while all her recycling still went into landfill. The council-supplied bin was so big she couldn't manoeuvre it, even when it was empty. Getting it to her gate for pick-up was impossible, as was cleaning it. She was terrified that if she tried to clean it, she would fall in and be cast there to die. The same day that I spoke to her, a gent told me that he got his bin to the kerb by leaning it over, tying it to the boot of his car, and towing it up his drive.

Inevitably, residents' surveys bring out the moaner. My heart sinks when a respondent says, 'Oh good, I've been wanting to do one of these; hang on while I make a drink and get comfy.' I brace myself for a long one, hoping that skill and patience will keep them on track.

There is occasionally a respondent who is so angry with their local council that they won't take part, not recognising that this is a confidential neutral opportunity for them to have their say.

The saddest interview I've ever done for a residents' survey was with a woman who insisted on taking part in the survey but was in tears. Her late husband had always dreamed of expanding their home business to provide more employment for family and local community members. He had needed to build a large shed, with appropriate resource consent for landscape change. In their area it was not possible to know what the total council costs would be until after the project was done. He had obtained a written estimate from council and budgeted an extra 15 per cent contingency just in case. Once built, the shed had done exactly as intended; the business had immediately started to grow, and he was looking to take on more staff.

However, the final bill from council arrived, and threw

everything into the air. It was more than $100,000 over what they could hope to afford, and more than double the council's original estimate. The husband was devastated, blaming himself since the whole project had been his dream. In the end, there were only two options available: to sell, which would mean losing their ancestral home also, or legally challenge council, with a real risk of losing and ending up with even more to pay. Without warning, her husband had taken a third, unthinkable, option, the only way out that would leave his wife and family financially intact. Suicide. His life insurance paid out, leaving his family freehold and all bills covered. All that poor lady wanted was her husband back.

Sometimes, when interviewing, it's important to turn off the clock, and just let the person at the other end of the phone vent. After that harrowing call, I took the rest of the evening off.

Then there was a woman, an owner of multiple businesses, who depended on a chauffeur/companion on a regular basis. This very organised-sounding woman used a mobility scooter for most daily movement, but the area she was able to use without assistance was very confined. She lives in a city known for its walking areas, wide open spaces, and beautiful parks and reserves. The area also has a large swimming pool complex. She loves to swim but is too scared to use the pools. She is unable to get out of the pools without assistance, or back into her scooter. The heavy doors at the pool made getting in and out of changing rooms completely impossible. She had asked the management if they could consult with mobility organisations to make the pools accessible for folk like her, but she was told that there was no budget.

The same lady found that some footpaths, parks and walkways were unavailable to her, due to surfaces, slopes or, even more simply, the bars or gates put in to prevent bikes and motor vehicles which also stopped her access. All she could do was watch her grandchildren from a distance as they enjoyed the facilities without her verbal support.

In another interview, the man I was listening to had been pleased I had called on behalf of his local council. Most folk will tell me about potholes or infrastructure issues which are causing problems, but this man was a moaner, with nothing positive to say about anything in his area. He told me about dangerous stormwater drains, potholes big enough for a car to fit in, wild dogs roaming the streets, raucous parties, and much more. It sounded like a shocking place to live, that clearly needed dealing with quickly. However, this man refused to share any information about which general vicinity, or even township, he was talking about. He was adamant that advising even broad location details would break his confidentiality and that council should be able to figure it out for themselves. He maintained that to find out where these issues were, all council had to do was ask the locals.

Isn't that exactly what council was doing by having me phone residents like him? My job has its frustrating elements.

During another survey, I was talking to a man who was being very abusive about his area health board. He was deeply upset that they did nothing for him; he lived in a remote area, and no one cared enough to visit him and make sure he was okay, health-wise. He lived with extended family some 60 kilometres from the nearest populated area and had never had a home visit. He was adamant that health care was a joke, and that he was part of the forgotten people, the ones who could not get any help or support. He said his GP had no idea of where he lived, of how he lived, his challenges and achievements, or of his family.

I was very surprised to learn, therefore, that he had a new pacemaker, and his wife was booked in for knee replacement surgery at the nearest public hospital. It was not enough; this man grieved the loss of personal contact, a shared cup of tea and companionable laughter with the health-care workers who attended him. He said he was a box to be ticked on a page of boxes, in some office where the workers had no faces or hearts. Where decisions were made by people who did not know him, too far away to see his eyes or feel his pain. Where they did not know what it meant for him, or his family, when they made those decisions. That they rudely addressed letters to him using his legal name, or no name at all, over information that used words he didn't understand. There was no one to tell him what the words meant, without him losing face, so he threw the letters away. Appointments came for 8.30 in the morning, when he had animals to feed, and 60 kilometres to travel. The health board didn't care he said, and he would not be interviewed.

Another surprise in the same survey was a man, 35 years old, who had no idea what vaccinations were. When I explained what they did, he was astounded that there was such a thing, and thought it was a fantastic idea, like something out of *Star Wars*. He wanted a list of what vaccinations there were available. It's not the first time that I've felt out of my depth.

11
Consents

Some local bodies audit their consent and licensing processes by getting feedback from folk who have received such a thing in the previous 12 months. These can range from food premises licences, dog registrations, building consents, resource consents, and manager's licences for bars, to commercial vessel licences. The interviewer phones named people to ask how they found the process, and if they think anything about it could have been done better.

Unfortunately, anything to do with local bodies can polarise people. One man I phoned hated council with a vengeance and was incredibly vocal about it, calling them all sorts of names. Naturally, I assumed he'd had a bad experience, yet when it came to the specific questions about the process, it was all fine, with no problems. However, he said quite clearly that one good experience was not going to change his view that they were all a dreadful lot in there and 'should be got rid of'.

Older folk often assume I am 'from the council' even

though I state quite clearly that I am calling on behalf of the council. This can lead to their telling me things that are outside my scope, but worse is when they ask me to resolve an issue for them. It's quite common for them to ask about what things can go into their recycling, or even what day the recycling is! As part of my preparation, I usually look up the council's phone number prior to starting interviewing, so that I can pass the number on. It costs nothing to be kind.

Dog registration queries can be fraught. Many folk are quite vocal that all they get for their money is a plastic tag, and they believe that registration penalises the good owners. It's not unusual to hear that the wandering and aggressive dogs are not registered anyway, so good owners believe they are paying for services that their dogs will never need. In these situations, the interview can turn from a five-minute call to double that when one of these owners really lets me have it, and it's hard to interrupt without causing further ill-feeling, as they want their grievance heard.

One lady who had got resource consent for a project had absolutely no memory of it, and she was very concerned that I had her name and contact details. Upon hearing that it was for a new shed, she was adamant that she had not got a new shed. I was becoming as perplexed as she was but persevered with trying to get to the bottom of the problem, mostly in an attempt to reassure her that I was legit. I asked her if she had undertaken any projects on her place recently, and she said no. This was sounding very odd, and I was getting desperate; there had to be an explanation. Then I asked her if there had been any building activity on her property recently, and she said no. I was about to give up, when she suddenly exclaimed, 'Oh, sorry dear, I've just seen it . . . you must be talking about the new garage I had put up. It's lovely, you know.' Problem solved.

§

With freedom camping coming under the spotlight so often in recent years, generally in a negative light, I was surprised when a motor camp owner went crook at me about their local council's attitude towards campgrounds trying to provide for self-contained camping. She owned an extensive camp which catered for almost everyone, from motel units to campsites, but was very frustrated as she had been blocked from offering an area with no facilities, other than perhaps taps and toilets. She had a spare piece of land which she wanted to make available to those campers who only required a place to park. She pointed out that self-contained motorhomes don't need kitchen or shower facilities, as they have their own, yet the council would not allow her to create an area for them, citing campground law. She was frustrated that councils were spending a lot of money on trying to find solutions to the freedom camping 'issue' but would not allow her to offer a safe and managed solution. Common sense could not prevail when up against the law.

Other calls just leave me shaking my head. One such was a gent who said he didn't know whether to laugh or cry. Getting a building consent for a shed on his bare block of land should have been totally straightforward, and it would have been, except for one thing. He had made the terrible mistake of not having any electrical certification included in the paperwork. Unable to supply a certificate, he had contacted his local council several times to try to sort out the mess, all to no avail. It was costing him time and money, and he felt boxed into a corner. Desperation was setting in. Eventually, with the help of a 'friendly' council employee, a solution was found — a solution which cost the landowner an extra $400. He had to get an electrical inspector to go to the site, inspect it, and provide the necessary documentation. At last, the certificate was accepted by council, and all was well. The problem, which left this poor fellow utterly gobsmacked, was that the site had no electricity to it, the building had no electrical fittings or wires installed (or intended), and there had been nothing for the inspector to inspect! But he got the certificate, and council was happy.

In another incident, a homeowner had decided that he needed an extension to his garage. After a lot of hard work and stress, the day came at last when the new concrete floor could be poured. At last, something tangible for all the outlay. Three cement-mixing trucks came, one after the other, and all hands were on deck for this exciting stage. Once the concrete was poured, the local building inspector came, and he used his trusty probe to test the concrete. The long-anticipated and hard-won concrete floor failed the probe test. The homeowner was devastated. What to do, and at whose cost? Would he have to have all that concrete taken out, only to start again? He couldn't begin to imagine who could do that type of work, or how much it would involve, in time or money. His blood pressure rising, he asked the inspector, 'Where to from here?' The inspector suggested that one of the council's engineers be asked to take a look at the new floor that same day. The homeowner grasped at the chance offered, though it was going to add $300 to his council account. That was better than a whole redo, surely? The engineer arrived a couple of hours later, just before knock-off time, with his own trusty test kit, which included a different type of probe to that of the building inspector's. The engineer took several readings, shook his head, and declared, 'I have no idea why I was called. This concrete is well within the guidelines.' The homeowner was so delighted, and knowing it was knock-off time, he offered the engineer a beer. Over the drink, they got chatting, naturally, about the engineer's work. He said he got called out almost daily to these kinds of rechecks, and they rarely failed. He reckoned that the probes the building inspectors used were cheap inferior types, and pretty useless. The homeowner couldn't help but think about the extra $300 it had cost him, working out that it would take him a full day's work to earn enough to cover that cost. All because the inspectors had inferior probes.

Some hairdressers work part-time, basing their workplace at home, fitting work around family life. Many purchase or hire a small movable cabin, placing it just a few steps from their house so that their business is separate from their private lives, while avoiding the time and expense of maintaining a shop.

One hairdresser, located in a small rural village, purchased a portable cabin, which is just one room, with a glassed entrance door taking up most of one end. The remaining three walls are completely lined and painted, with hairdressing equipment on shelves, a wall adorned with a large mirror for client use, and a small desk for her computer and administration requirements. The single room is bright, spacious and very neat.

Imagine her surprise when the local council inspector refused to issue her an approval to conduct her business there as she did not have an exit sign above the door. She pointed out to him that there was only one door, which took up all of one end of the building, and that her clients could only gain entry via that door, so surely they would know it was the exit, but this inspector was not to be persuaded. The door needed an exit sign. She offered to draw up a hand-made exit sign while he waited, but no; it had to be a proper sign, commercially produced, in appropriate colouring to ensure it was easy to spot in a fire. She was fairly certain that if they could see the sign, they would probably also spot the door underneath it, but again no, he was not to be persuaded.

Once she had travelled to town (30 kilometres each way) to get the sign, she installed it, then contacted the inspector and offered to send him a photo, in the hope of saving time and money. She was mistaken; he insisted on driving out to inspect the sign, despite it taking nearly two hours out of his day, not to mention the cost of running the council's car. She got her certification but is left wondering how the inspector thought her clients would have left the building if there was no sign.

§

I love circuses, but not the interviewing kind. For one consent feedback survey, I had randomly selected the required number of potential interviewees and, as the actual interview would be taking less than five minutes in most cases, I was looking forward to it. So, there I was at my workspace on a lovely sunny afternoon, thinking I'll have this one done before you've had time to sneeze.

First on the list, disconnected number. Replace it.

Second on the list, never heard of the guy. Incorrect number. Replace it.

Third... Mum's out for the afternoon. Call back.

Fourth... just going to collect his grandson. Call back.

Fifth on the list. 'Oh no, we didn't do the consent, the builder did.' Get his number. Phone him. 'No, it was the draughtsman.' Get his number. Call him. 'No, it was the project manager.' Get his number. Call him. 'Good heavens, no! It was the homeowner.' That was the person I'd called in the first place. Oh dear. It took three very long days to complete that 'simple' job.

12

Surprises!

Approaching the back of the 1950s ex-state house, I was not surprised to see concrete steps leading up to a covered-in, small wooden porch. Three doors beckoned off the porch. To the left was the main entry, with a doormat under its wooden step, shoes lined up beside it, and a doorbell on the frame.

To the right was an open doorway with free-hanging vinyl ribbon waving in the breeze, screening what was presumably the laundry. Between the kitchen and laundry doorways was what appeared to be a hallway door.

Going up the concrete steps, I approached the kitchen door and pressed the bell. A noise from the laundry startled me, and I turned to see the totally bare, bent-over, pink bottom of an entirely naked thirty-something man loading clothes into a front-loader washing machine.

He clearly had no idea that I was there, but I was hopelessly trapped. If I moved he may hear me; no way did I want him to know that I had seen him in his morning glory.

Desperately silent, I inched my way across the porch,

eyes riveted on his head, willing him to not turn around.

Slowly, slowly, I made my way down the steps until out of view, finally chancing on breathing again.

Then, to make my presence known (I still needed the interview), I coughed loudly. There was scrambling in the laundry, then a head popped around the doorway.

'Yes, can I help you?' he enquired, firmly keeping most of his body out of view.

I explained what I was there for. 'Just a minute,' he said, and soon he appeared in a dressing gown, and we did the interview. Should our paths ever cross again, I will never ever let on to this lad the truth of that morning!

§

The very smart new townhouse stood out among its older neighbours. It had clean square lines, low-maintenance gardens with neatly trimmed shrubs, gravelled areas, water fountain bubbling away and a serenity reminiscent of Japanese styles; it was truly beautiful. The elderly lady who invited me in was quick and alert, and I interviewed her in an elegantly furnished room which had mementoes of her lifetime of travels to all corners of the globe.

The interview passed quickly; she was concise, consistent and quite clear, and I was pleased to have completed the interview in a mutually efficient manner. As we returned to her entrance foyer, this dear lady paused to show me a handcrafted wall-hanging that was just inside the front entrance. She was obviously quite proud of the hanging, explaining its origins to me in quite some detail. The interlude that we stood side by side looking at the hanging would have been around five minutes, and I had no inkling of what was to come.

Having shown me her treasured hanging, she took my arm, firmly steering me towards the room we had just come from, and she said, quite clearly and innocently, 'Now dear, I see you are doing a survey, so let's get on with it.' It was clear that she had no memory of the previous half-hour. Meekly I sat down, asked her just enough questions to keep it real, and then left her happily sure she'd contributed well.

§

Sunday afternoon, and the house door is answered by a Catholic priest. Explaining what I was there for, and assuming he wouldn't want to be disturbed on his sacred day, I offered to make an appointment for during the week.

'No, no,' he replied. 'Come in; you may just be the answer to my prayers. God works in many ways.'

I had no idea how I could be an answer to anyone's prayers, but in I went, relieved to not have to make a return trip.

Almost through the interview, all was going smoothly, when I asked him about local infrastructure like footpaths, water, sewerage and the like. Unexpectedly, he laughed, slapped his knee and then said, 'Thank you my dear, I knew you were the answer.'

I had no idea what he was talking about. He picked up his well-worn Bible from the table and searched quickly, until he found the line he wanted, Matthew 3:3 — '... make his path straight.'

That priest's whole demeanour changed as he was

suddenly gripped by a new excitement, clearly anxious to get his thoughts onto paper. Finishing the interview as unobtrusively as possible, I left him to get on with his sermon, but not before he apologised, explaining that later the same day he had to address a congregation he didn't know, and he'd been getting increasingly stressed that no topic he came up with had felt right, until now.

God really does work in mysterious ways!

13
Animals

Two very large dog bowls on the homeowner's front porch, along with a wide black studded collar hanging by the door, provided good reason to pause before entering the gate. Large bowls equal large dogs, and studded collars don't exactly suggest gentle quiet types. I was intruding on a dog's territory; there could be a penalty. Where was that dog, and just how hungry? I wasn't keen to be today's leading news story. 'Woman becomes dog's lunch' has no appeal at all.

I called out 'Hello,' in the hope that someone would come to the door, or that the dog would show itself. Who knows? It could be friendly.

No interviewer-eating set of jaws appeared, nor was there any barking. I opened the gate, my senses on full alert, searching anxiously in case the beast was lurking in ambush. My heart was beating hard and fast, despite the fact that I was holding my breath.

Knocking on the door is always the toughest moment; there's wisdom in the proverb that you should let sleeping dogs lie. There was no answering bark. This is my worst nightmare. If they bark, at least you know where the dog is, so you have some warning. The silent dog is the most dangerous. Footsteps approached, thankfully human. The lady who opened the door was keen to be interviewed, but I couldn't respond freely as I was still fretting about the unknown beast. As casually as I could muster, in an effort to find out just how much danger I was in, I asked her what the absent dog's name was. Laughing, she explained, 'There is no dog. Those bowls are my privacy strategy; they are there to deter unsolicited visitors like salesmen and surveys. They work really well; most people don't even come in the gate!'

On another occasion I was interviewing a lovely elderly gent who had a little dog companion he was besotted with. It was nipping at my legs, inflicting real pain, but the gent firmly believed it was just playing. The malevolent look in that dog's eye, guarding his owner from my intrusion, made me thankful it wasn't any bigger. Understanding the dog's protective instinct neither excused the biting nor neutralised the pain. I was trapped, unable to respond appropriately without distressing the owner.

Partway through the interview, the gent excused himself to go to the toilet. In his absence, the dog was on guard. The message was clear: move and you die.

Suddenly, it rushed at my leg again, but, with the owner out of the room, I grasped my chance. As the attacker sunk its teeth into my left leg, my right foot shot underneath the dog, lifting it off the floor. I grabbed the dog by the scruff of the neck, plonking it on my knee.

Taking care to keep those sharp teeth at a safe distance, I started stroking him, talking quietly. The words may not have been very polite, but the tone was caring and nurturing. Even 'you little sod' can sound endearing in the right tone. That wee dog was so angry, shaking tension poured out of its very tight wee body. The low growl was unmistakably menacing.

With no way of knowing what would happen next, I was not letting go until I had to. When I heard the gent flush the toilet, I carefully placed the dog back on the floor, facing it away from my legs. It spent the rest of my visit circling me with a fixed glare, growling constantly, but not once did it touch or attack, thank goodness.

Dogs are a mixed blessing. Most are lovely, but I cannot forget that I am a stranger invading their territory. It is folly to ignore 'Beware of the dog' signs, or the totally still dog that's growling from inside the gate. Avoiding looking a dog in the eye is difficult but essential, as the direct stare can equate to a challenge in their minds. Letting them sniff me is important, especially as their noses inform them that I've been to some interesting places and may have met other dogs.

Dogs have brought me toys, asked for a scratch, slobbered all over me and my paperwork, jumped in my car, rested their soulful eyes on my lap, peed on my leg as though I was a tree, and totally ignored me by sleeping through the whole visit.

At one reasonably remote house no one answered my knock, but when I turned to leave there was a large dog between me and the gate, standing guard. He had arrived silently and stood with his hackles raised. Each time I took a step, even sideways, he bared his teeth and growled. I was totally trapped. It was going to be a long day. I hoped for an unlikely passer-by to rescue me, to no avail, but fortunately the owners arrived before long. They praised the dog, laughing to me about how wonderfully their training was working. Then they rewarded him with a dog treat. I am left wondering what will happen when it's an unaccompanied child who knocks on their door.

Who owns which dog can be a surprise. There was the frail elderly widow with the German shepherd she couldn't bear to part with, as it was the last link to her beloved late husband. She struggled to take it for walks but was determined to continue. The dog's good training was the single factor to making the relationship work. Then there was the tough businessman whose little chihuahua turned him to jelly. The joy is that most of the dogs out there are loved and well cared for.

This is not always the case. At a small unit in a block of retirement flats, an elderly woman invited me into her lounge. In front of the heater lay the fattest dog I've ever seen. The poor thing could hardly move, and he was panting. He looked like a terrier of some kind, but it was hard to be sure. Great rolls of fat stretched his skin so tightly that surely a pin would pop him. His 'mother', as she called herself, was very proud of this dog. She had knitted him some woolly jackets and something akin to gloves for his feet. The poor wee thing didn't go outside any more. The owner said that he preferred to stay inside. I could see why, as when he tried to walk it was a painful waddle, like watching a dog version of a 400-kilo person, and unbearable. The owner had a bowl of treats by her chair, and every few minutes she would feed him another treat for being a good boy. He was the most miserable dog I've ever seen, with dull eyes and quick light breaths.

The next day I called the SPCA about him, which is highly irregular, but I was really bothered. The girl on the other end of the phone asked me if the dog was fed, dry, warm and loved. I tried to say 'yes, but' and explain, but she was not interested, saying that obesity was not cruelty, just misinformed love. I remain appalled by that response and firmly believe that this little dog's life was painful and cruel. Killing with kindness and loving it to death really is a thing. Thankfully, of all the hundreds I've met over the years, that wee dog is the only animal who left me deeply upset about the owner's treatment.

Other animal encounters are just plain hilarious. At one home, the impending interview appeared to be straightforward. I'd knocked on the door and subsequently explained to the polite friendly lady what I was there for. She was the sole occupant of the 1960s home where she and her late husband had raised their family. She kindly invited me in, to work at her sunny dining table, while she sat opposite, open and ready.

I explained the survey again, then asked her the first question, only to be completely blindsided by a deep voice from the corner of the room asking, 'What are you thinking?'

Turning, I saw a large elderly parrot-like bird looking at me with his head tilted, as though awaiting an answer.

'Hello,' I said, not very imaginatively.

'Hello yourself,' he replied.

The lady laughed and told 'Harry' to pipe down.

I asked the question again, and, before the lady could reply, Harry said, 'Mind your own bloody business.'

That was just the start of one of the most bizarre and disconcerting half-hours I've ever endured. Harry kept up a full barrage throughout, swearing, repeating our words, and asking questions at the top of his voice, while his owner completely ignored him, even when he used language that I'm certain she would never use. I really struggled to keep my composure, torn between dismay, professionalism and the desire to laugh hysterically.

At the end of the interview, as I was leaving, I turned to him and said, 'Bye Harry,' to which he replied in a sullen voice, 'Fuck off.' His owner never even batted an eyelid.

Cats are an interesting element to an interviewer's day. There's the disappearing cat with big saucer eyes who decides I am definitely that cat-kidnapper he'd been warned about and promptly vanishes.

Opposite him is the smoocher, who purrs all over me for the entire interview, dribbling onto my clothes and papers and generally being a pest.

Then there's the stealth-attack cat, which appears to be friendly, but when I get close enough, zap! A set of claws or teeth separate the pores of my skin. I can't react as dear little moggy is 'just playing'. Last, there's the dead cat. He can be anywhere, spread out, eyes shut, breathing deeply, clearly not interested in any interviewer, not moving, nothing. His day is far too busy for the likes of me.

I got caught out once by a horse. I'm a well-experienced horse person, so I didn't expect any issues from a horse grazing in the section around the house that I was to visit. The house windows were open, and I was optimistic that someone was home. The horse was friendly; I let it sniff me before I went in the gate, and I observed all the usual strange-horse protocols: giving it a pat before walking purposefully to the door while avoiding any proximity to the horse's back end. I didn't fall for the 'I'm starving' entreaty either. No one was home, so I turned to exit the property. That was when I learnt that the horse was working off a different manual than mine.

As I went to leave, the horse blocked my way. Apparently, it required a rub on its back in payment of the gate toll. The problem was, of course, that the horse's idea of how long a rub should take, and my personal view on the matter, were different. This horse clearly thought it had booked a full deep body massage, not just a little rub. Added to my concern, the horse was in its moulting season, so great clumps of hair were coming off, covered with residue dirty powder which was finding its way not only onto my hands but also breezing onto my clothes. I appreciate the relief that the horse was receiving but was not particularly keen to be the masseuse for long. While I was giving it a rub, I manoeuvred myself to the gate side of the horse, then left with as much dignity as I could muster. It was hard to know if the eyes boring into my back were doleful or laughing at me.

Walking from one house to another on a sweltering-hot day, I wasn't surprised to see every possible window open on the next house. Heat is not just the interviewer's nightmare, on days when any breeze is welcome. For me, dehydration can sneak up unnoticed, if I work continuously.

On this day, I suddenly became aware of a low hum in the air. A huge swirl of swarming bees was descending on both me and the front yard of a wee house that had young children's toys spread around. Every window of the house was wide open, and I assumed that the young family were inside, oblivious to the impending danger bearing down on their home. A swarm of bees flying into a home could have drastic consequences, especially if there was a baby in bed somewhere, or a child allergic to bees.

For a second I was conflicted. Should I jump into my car for safety or battle through the swarm to make the homeowner aware of the danger? I froze, unsure. What would they think of a stranger barging into their home? That street's inhabitants are mostly folk with English as their second language, so would they understand the urgency, or maybe think they were being attacked by a crazy woman? A few minutes later, sitting safely in my car, I was relieved to see the swarm start to move off, rising over the wee house and away, but not before a rogue bee, running late, injected a sting into a poor unsuspecting Lycra-clad cyclist who happened to pass by at just the wrong moment.

14
Weather

The day was turning into a nightmare. I was working to a tight deadline, so had no choice but to work in the rain. Arriving at someone's door dripping wet, expecting to be invited in, is way beyond reasonable. I was desperately trying to keep the paperwork dry, but it was proving almost impossible. The wind, and the fact that I didn't have a free hand, made an umbrella useless. Try ringing a doorbell or opening a latched garden gate while holding paperwork and an umbrella.

Rain brings puddles and slippery paths, so my feet were soon soaking wet, and a broken ankle very plausible. The only good thing was that householders were home, and open to diversion.

I arrived at one home, however, very cold and wet, and was pleased to find a sheltered porch to stand in. I rang the doorbell and the lady answered. She was pleased to agree to do the interview, so the day was looking up, until she stepped forward onto the porch, firmly closing the house door behind her. The porch was not big enough for two, so I was forced to step back out into the rain, and there I stood for the next 20 minutes, getting thoroughly rained on, while she stayed nicely dry under cover, answering my questions.

Conversely, hot summer days suck the liquid out as I walk the streets and, truth be told, potential respondents are probably at the beach anyway, or resting somewhere, trying to cool off. None of these folk are remotely interested in being diverted from their precious weekend by a dehydrated and desperate-looking interviewer who's clutching a clipboard.

15
Family strings

I am wary of insulting cultural beliefs or trampling on how a person likes to be treated. For example, no matter the state of the house, I always offer to take my shoes off before stepping inside, unless it's unsafe. Most people say not to worry, but they appreciate the offer. Similarly, it can be very important not to 'rock the boat', for the sake of an individual's well-being.

Approaching a unit at the far end of a communal driveway, I was struck by how beautiful it was. The unit's brown and red trims were offset by a profusion of garden colour and contrasting leaf types, all immaculately kept. Two Ferrari-red muscle cars gleamed in the parking spaces, clearly someone's pride and joy.

Hearing the quiet hum of an electric lawnmower, I followed the path around to the side of the unit and found a frail-looking elderly woman carefully mowing. There was a well-tended vegetable garden, where everything was in neat rows, not a weed in sight, and fruit bushes neatly trimmed for the small amount of space available. It was a garden to be proud of.

The lady herself was barely five feet tall, and despite being in jeans, she gave the impression of immaculate presentation, with short well-styled hair and just a touch of make-up. She was very thin, however, which made her seem tiny.

I was a bit puzzled about the muscle cars out front, as I certainly couldn't imagine she would be able to see over the dashboard, let alone drive them!

She was friendly and enquiring, so we very quickly got through the respondent selection process, ascertaining that it was her son, who lived with her, that I needed to speak to.

At that point, her demeanour changed to what could only be described as outright fear. She began to shake and, almost in tears, she begged me to leave him undisturbed as he was asleep. She said he didn't like being woken up, and she couldn't bear to make him angry. This poor lady was reduced to a terrified miserable mouse at the very thought.

Looking for a way to resolve the situation in a way that would help her feel better, I double-checked that he lived there permanently, and she replied in a voice so deeply sad that it broke my heart. He had moved in with her a couple of years beforehand, after the break-up of his marriage, to 'look after her', even though she hadn't wanted or needed it.

As she was so distressed, I was quick to reassure her that I would never ask for someone to be woken up (which is the truth) and that I'd leave it for now. She was appallingly relieved. Then I asked her if she was okay, at which she drew herself up and defiantly said, 'Of course

I am.' She went on to add, 'My son loves me. I should be grateful. He's not all bad.'

An interesting but sad choice of words.

Sometimes an interview is not achieved for a reason that I heartily agree with, creating personal difficulty, as I am torn between trying to persuade the respondent and letting it go because I personally believe he's right. One such was during a telephone survey, and I was partway through cold calling when I dialled his number.

A man barked at me, down the phone, with a strong warrior voice, deep and compelling. 'You want to talk to me? What for?'

I explained that the local council wanted to hear residents' views about the infrastructure in their area.

'So you come up here and talk to me, in my house, to my face,' he said.

I replied that I didn't live in his area, which is why I had phoned. He wasn't having a bar of it.

'Up here, we talk face to face,' he said. 'If you really want to know what I think, then you come and visit me. We drink together, eat together, then I will answer your questions. I'm not telling you what I think of our reserves or rubbish collection until I can see your eyes. Then I will know if you are really listening, or if you are just ticking some boxes on a piece of paper so someone can say that Council listened. Do you know what listening is? It's taking time, eating and sitting together, and showing respect. Leave your clock behind and sit with me for as long as it takes to hear what I want to say. I need to see your face so I know I can trust you.'

Sadly, I had to decline his invitational challenge, and

so he wouldn't be interviewed. He was right of course; I was working with an agenda and timeframe that were not his, and they did not fit with his culture. If he had done the interview, my needs would have been met, but not his, making it a one-sided relationship — taking with no giving. With all the technology available, I couldn't do the one thing that ensures real communication: sit down together and talk, properly talk.

At one home it was other people's treatment of a young Kiwi lass which delayed my work. When I arrived, the girl I was hoping to interview was deeply upset by an incident which had happened to her earlier the same day, and she was in no mood for any interaction with strangers like me. At the door, I acknowledged how upset she looked, by asking if she was okay, at which point she burst into tears. Putting down my paperwork, I reached over to her and asked, more gently, whether there was something I could do. Sometimes the human response is more important than achieving an interview.

This lass was about 18 years old, very slim in jeans and sweater, and had Asian features, including short, straight, black hair.

Her story came out in bits, as she tried to settle her tears.

Earlier in the day she had gone shopping, all excited because she had been given a voucher to a clothing store she'd never been in before. It was a rare experience, to have the funds for buying something brand new, and she was looking forward to exploring what the store might offer.

At this point in her story, I was wondering what on

earth could have gone wrong. Maybe the voucher was out of date, or maybe there was nothing in her size, though that was difficult to imagine.

She had been in the shop, thoroughly enjoying the sheer pleasure of looking at the styles and colours on offer, and had finally settled on three items she wished to try on. No one had approached her to assist, despite the fact that there were staff talking among themselves at the counter. She had noticed several glances her way, but each time she had tried to catch someone's eye, the assistants had turned away, which had left her feeling a bit puzzled.

As she approached the counter to say that she would like to try on the chosen garments, the shop manager had looked her straight in the eye, and said very loudly, and slowly, as though to an idiot, 'DO . . . YOU . . . SPEAK . . . ENGLISH?'

The lass had been mortified, as other shoppers turned to stare, and she explained to me how exposed and isolated she felt. She had dropped the items on the counter and fled; her lovely gift had been completely crushed by the manager's words.

This lass is a sixth-generation Kiwi, with one great-great-grandfather who came from China and who she happens to resemble. She said that being treated like an alien isn't that uncommon, but on this day, when she had just been a Kiwi teenager enjoying a morning out, it had got on top of her. She wanted to know if she would ever be accepted in this country as belonging here. I had no words; there is nothing I can say which will overcome the very real experience of prejudicial assumptions and racist stereotyping that the ignorant still use. How sad that the manager did not at least give the girl a chance to speak. Then, if there had indeed turned out to be a language barrier, it could have been handled much more discreetly than this.

Over the years, I have come across many variations of this story, where folk who are not Pakeha get treated as potential shoplifters, as butts of jokes or as idiots. I do not understand why any of my fellow New Zealanders would do this.

I enjoy seeing folk celebrating their heritage, and one day I got the loveliest glimpse of this, quite unexpectedly. About lunchtime, in a relatively new subdivision of low-maintenance homes set in streets with wide berms, tree plantings and green areas, I was walking along counting the houses (interviewing in every fifth house) when I noticed a fabulous sight on the other side of the street. A large multi-generational family was having lunch in their garage, with the roller door fully up, exposing their activities to the passer-by. This was no ordinary lunch nor ordinary family. They were dressed in the colourful costumes of their homeland, with elegant white robes and hats adorned with gold and red patterns. Even the children were dressed smartly, and I noticed that every person sat up very straight, with an almost regal air. The table was laden with food, and the smells wafting across the street made me very hungry indeed. There was talk and laughter, and the thing I noticed was that not one of those family looked out onto the street; they were relaxed and comfortable, completely absorbed in what they were doing as though the rest of the world wasn't there. I was enveloped by the sight, and smells, and did not want to move on. How I admired their strength as a group, celebrating their differences without fear or self-consciousness.

New Zealand is such a diverse community, with a wide variety of activities and interests, yet we are bound by common threads. Over the years, I have come to understand that most of us aspire to be active, to be loved, to achieve whatever we see as important.

16
Finding that cross-section

One thing that strikes me time and again is the great ideas that folk have. Respondents often put forward well-considered solutions to issues; they have obviously been thinking of ways forward in some depth. Of course, the other side of that is the occasional uninformed person who just wants to sack everybody in power and get rid of bureaucracy in any form. They are entitled to their views, just like the rest of us.

When working in an area, it's important to make sure that every street, track and city building is checked for a dwelling, to ensure a fair sample and representation. Sometimes I find a lived-in caravan behind a business, or a sleep-out being used by a renter. Keeping my eyes open, while trying not to appear nosey, is key.

It's quite common for a person to continue gardening, or working on a project, while being interviewed. Whatever makes the respondent comfortable, as long as it's legal and safe, is fine by me.

People tell interviewers amazing information that they really shouldn't share with a stranger, including personal details, family history, funny stories. It takes a lot of skill and tact to keep to the job at hand sometimes, and to get the interview done as quickly as is reasonable, without causing offence.

Regardless of whether they agree to the interview or not, I always try to leave a good impression, in order to lift their day. On a cold, wet late afternoon when there's just one interview left to be achieved, a refusal can be the last straw, but I try to thank them anyway, and smile; maybe another day they'll be more helpful to some other interviewer.

Sometimes it can be challenging...

The businesswoman facing me at her door was angry; her hands punctuated every point as she spat her thoughts at me. My crime had been to ask to speak to a male member of the household. She was deeply offended, giving me no chance to explain. In full flight she went on and on about equality, about how everyone's voice needs to be heard, not just men's, her opinions count too, sexism in the modern world; the whole shebang.

When she finally paused for a breath, I empathised, but went on to explain that we have a quota of male and female to ensure that the survey represented the population; on this job I had got way out of kilter, having interviewed 19 women and only two men, so I was looking for men to interview in order to even it up a little.

She then sailed into me again, reinvigorated in her attack, saying that who cares if more women than men are interviewed, why shouldn't that be okay? Women could answer on behalf of the population just as well as any man could. She obviously saw no irony at all in her assertion that while men couldn't answer for her, she could answer for men. Equity or equality were clearly only the right of women, in her view, rather than a human right applicable to both genders.

Looking for a particular age can cause some interesting issues. Knocking on over 20 doors to find a young man, when I am a middle-aged woman, has the potential to turn into farce, and requires strict adherence to the script. Most people pick up on it with humour, with the occasional elderly woman even suggesting that if I find a suitable young man perhaps I could send him her way. It seems odd that this should be acceptable behaviour, whereas if an elderly gent said this about a young woman it would be deemed creepy and could land him in a great deal of trouble.

Sometimes people are surprised at who I will interview. Outside a city apartment, one of a block which had been converted from a motel complex, I was interviewing a man with special needs about his use of public transport, when I was accosted by a very angry woman. She was adamant intellectually impaired people should not be included in surveys, stating quite clearly, in his hearing, that 'handicapped' people couldn't possibly give proper answers, and that she was going to complain. This lady was employed as a support worker for the folk living in that block. The respondent got a little distressed about her interference, but I reassured him that his opinion was indeed valid and, despite her objections, we carried on. That young man had some very clear views about public transport. His nearest bus stop was at a place where the footpath was quite narrow, and he explained that he didn't feel safe standing waiting for the bus, as cyclists brushed past him on the footpath, making him afraid, so each day he walked a great distance to the next stop, where the path was wider and safer for him. He also pointed out that he couldn't attend some evening events he was interested in, like sports games, as there was no way for him to get safely back home afterwards, due to bus timetables. Unlike his 'support' worker, I believe that this young man, as a member of society, has the right to express his concerns, just as everyone else does.

17
Connections

One man I had the pleasure of sitting down with gave me a personal gift I shall always treasure.

From the footpath, beautiful black wrought-iron gates supported by richly coloured brickwork columns invited me into a wide driveway bordered with neatly spaced trees, sweeping lawns and comprehensive gardens. Birdsong accompanied my approach to an elegant New England-style homestead.

I was nervous of the inevitable dogs; places like this always have a pack of large dogs that bound up. The question was, would they be friend or foe?

Deep chimes pealed through the house when I pressed the doorbell. I half-expected a white-gloved servant to answer. To my surprise, a very elderly gent opened the door, and once he had established my mission, he warmly invited me in.

I was struck by his keen mind but, more importantly, his gentle well-established aura of graciousness, like his home. He answered my questions efficiently, so we were done in very short order. He then asked me about myself; there was something compelling about him that invited conversation.

Putting aside my work, I then thoroughly enjoyed the observations and opinions of this well-travelled businessman and philanthropist. We talked about his town, politics, history and family. Eventually, the dots connected and I realised that I was already aware of some of his story, due to the family's high community profile. To be invited to spend one-on-one time with this amazing, yet physically fragile, gentleman was a complete honour.

When he asked about my married surname (it's common to the area), I took the opportunity to ask him how much he knew of his family's earlier history, from the 1860s to 1960s period, explaining that I was uncertain in regard to my own ancestors' history, which may be linked to his own family.

Upon hearing the name of my ancestor, this lovely man proceeded to fill in so many blanks for me, just off the top of his head! He also told me where I may find relevant photos in public archives (I did), and about the two families' business connections. I was awestruck by his total recall and his generosity in sharing so freely. I left his home feeling utterly blessed, knowing that I had been in the presence of someone very, very special.

Sadly, only a few weeks later, I read of his passing. The funeral was huge apparently, with dignitaries from New Zealand and abroad, with many fine speeches. I didn't go; our interlude together had given me much joy, leaving me thoughtful, inspired and blessed. Treasured moments indeed.

A similar connection had happened some years earlier, with another gent. One evening I was phoning residents in a Northland area, asking them their opinion of their local council's performance regarding infrastructure, reserves, facilities and the like.

An elderly man was trying to explain an issue he had and asked me if I knew the area at all. I admitted to knowing a little, as my late grandfather had lived there and shown me around some years before.

The gent asked me who my grandfather was, and when I told him, we both got the loveliest surprise. They had been workmates and best friends at the local dairy factory. This gent went on to tell me stories about my grandfather, stories I'd never heard before. I learnt such a lot from that unexpected connection. The only blight was that I couldn't record the gent's personal details to get in touch with him again; respondent confidentiality is guaranteed, even when the circumstances suggest that it would probably be fine. However, I remain ever grateful for the stories he shared.

More recently, in another area, a hot windy Saturday morning found me randomly picking houses to approach for a quick five-minute questionnaire on behalf of the local council. Being close to lunchtime, I was getting desperate for a drink, shade and some lunch, but I decided to do just one more interview before taking a break.

An elderly lady answered the door, inviting me in. With such a short questionnaire I'd normally just stand at the threshold, but this lady looked a bit fragile on her feet so, out of consideration for her, in I went.

Lying on her table was a photograph of an ancestor of

mine! I was so surprised that I couldn't help asking about it. Astonishingly, it turned out that she was descended from the same person; we shared a Scottish ancestor from the 1820s. I put the interview aside, and we had a lively half-hour sharing information and stories from both the New Zealand and Scottish links.

The lady asked for my contact details, which I gave her, and I have since sent her some information that she requested. It's a small world, as they say, and when out interviewing who's to know what surprise waits to bless my day?

18
Interviewers

From time to time there is a need to add an extra one or two interviewers to my team. Most of the time I can cover the local work myself, and there is a small but willing band who make themselves available if needed. However, every now and then a bigger job comes along which necessitates extra interviewers. The criteria for suitability are fairly straightforward, including fluency in English (written and oral), an ability to meet deadlines, self-motivation, own vehicle, driver's licence and being able to get along with a wide range of people. Map reading skills also help.

When prospective interviewers turn up for their own interview, they have about 10 seconds to make the first impression. After all, out in the field that is how long it takes for a respondent to have a gut reaction, which often decides the outcome of the interviewer's approach. So why would a job seeker turn up late, or reeking of cigarette smoke, or with their phone buzzing in their hands? One applicant's vocabulary stretched to using mild swear words at least twice in every sentence! Then there was the man who called me 'darling' every time he spoke. Needless to say, none of the above were taken on.

Most applicants are lovely, and it comes down to whether they really can work evenings and weekends, and their confidence with strangers, dogs and driving in areas they don't know. There is also the X-factor; do they project respect, empathy and confidence.

I once had a salutary lesson in dress code. Working in an area on a cold day, I grabbed a jersey from the back of the car that was not a work item. It was clean and tidy but not smart. At the first four houses I was refused at the door. Thinking about it, and wondering why, since it had never happened before, I changed the jersey to my work one, and had no more refusals all day. I was the same person, with the same approach, yet wearing the wrong jersey can make all the difference. Lesson learned.

Interviewers, like anyone in personal-contact roles, need to be able to adapt their voice to match the respondent.

§

The 30-something gent who answered the door one afternoon was very softly spoken, in contrast to his three-year-old daughter who bounced her exciting news that it was nearly her birthday, and would I like to come to her party? I regretfully declined, explaining that I would be working that day.

While interviewing her dad I slowed my speaking pace slightly and dropped my voice so as to more closely reflect his, thereby reducing the contrast between our speaking styles. He had suffered a stroke, and words did not come easily. Folk can become irritated or feel threatened when interviewers don't match the respondent's demeanour. A clipped speaker does not respect or appreciate a casual take-your-time interviewer and, conversely, a person who speaks slowly can feel overpowered, bullied or simply inadequate when confronted by a businesslike interviewer. The wording of the interview doesn't change, just the delivery style. This also works on the phone, so 'reading' the respondent's voice is a very helpful skill.

However, the greeting on the phone does change to reflect how the person on the other end answered. There is no point saying 'Good morning' to someone who has answered 'Hi' as the formality can put them on edge or make them wary, just as saying 'Hi' to someone who answered their phone with 'Good morning' may make them feel that I am assuming a familiarity that's not there.

Phone interviewing can find me pressing the handset hard into my ear or trying to hold the phone as far away as possible. Some folk speak so quietly they are almost whispering, making their responses difficult to get. However, there's also the yeller. He (yes, it's always a he) just about blasts my eardrums out, usually because he hasn't put his hearing aids in.

One guy yelled at me all the way through an interview, despite not having a hearing impairment. The odd thing was, he only had good things to say about the topic at hand, and even made a couple of jokes, but it was all at the top of his voice. I was so shattered by the end of the interview that I had to take a break, and Panadol, to regain my equilibrium.

§

Security is a big part of the job. If the material holds private information, rather than just general opinions, after each interview I lock the completed paperwork in my car, making sure that it can't be seen by the casual passer-by. Respondents' confidentiality is paramount. In fact, if the interview has very sensitive material, it gets locked in the car boot for added protection.

I was already committed to approaching the very comfortable-looking 1980s home high up on a hillside, having trudged my way up a steep stone-wall-lined driveway, when I realised that the homeowner had friends around for a BBQ. Beers in hand, music quietly playing, they were clearly having an afternoon of talk and laughter. The food laid out on the table looked amazing, with fresh breads, salads and dips. What's more, the BBQ was smoking delicious smells into the air that sucked at my poor starving stomach with treacherous promise. A man in his forties called out: 'Hello?'

Embarrassed at having intruded, I explained what I was there for, and offered to come back another day. What I didn't quite understand was why they all burst out laughing when I said who I was and where from. The gent then asked me questions about the survey, in a way that I thought was a little more detailed than most folk do. He wanted to know not only who it was for, when the results would be out, would they be public, how had I chosen his house, and what was its purpose, but also what would happen if he said no? I answered all his questions, but then he told me not to come back as he wouldn't be taking part. I tried to persuade him, explaining how important it was and so on, but still he refused. There was no tension in his words, so I was a little puzzled; usually I can sense why the respondent doesn't want to join in, and often I can mitigate that, but not in this case.

Finally, one of the women said to him, 'Come clean, tell her the truth.'

I looked at him, waiting, but with no idea what she was talking about. He laughed, then said he wouldn't be taking part because he was the client; the person who oversaw the feedback/survey process on behalf of the council I was doing the work for. My heart sank. I was certain that this would be when my boss would hear that they had lost all future contracts due to something I did wrong. The gent must have understood what I was thinking, because he said, 'Don't worry, you did great. Might even recommend you get a pay rise for your sterling job.' I was delighted, of course, but it served to remind me that we should assume everyone could be the client. You just never know where they lurk.

19
Other types of surveys

During a period when I was unable to commit to the hours required by market research companies, I undertook ad hoc private work for local businesses and branches, gathering and evaluating feedback from their clients, on a confidential basis.

One person who signed up was the regional manager of a national company. He was very upset with sweeping changes rolled out by his head office, so he contracted me to canvass long-standing clients regarding their experiences of the changes. He was convinced that the outcome would be widespread dissatisfaction, so he planned to present the results at the company's next board meeting, in order to get the detrimental changes reversed.

Unfortunately for him, the responses showed almost 100 per cent support for the changes. Clients had even suggested additional ideas to develop the new systems further; he angrily responded that he would not be passing on any of the results or suggestions. I understand that he resigned from the company soon afterwards. Quality research discovers what people are thinking, so the risk is high that it will not support any preconceived personal agenda.

Some organisations use online surveys. There are many risks involved when taking this path. Generally, the questions are not peer-reviewed for quality, the providers usually do not belong to a national ethics body, and there is no requirement to meet the industry standard of 65 per cent minimum response rate. For a company's board to accept, and make decisions, based on any online survey of current clients for which they may have received less than 5 per cent response seems extraordinary. Online surveys are usually answered by folk who have an issue or those feeling generous with their time. The surveys tend to be simplistic, and they are devoid of probing for clarification or picking up on tone to identify underlying issues, so there is no real understanding gained of what the respondent thinks. Busy going-ahead folk generally won't bother completing online surveys, yet they are probably the very people who companies need to be listening to, in order to properly enhance future service.

I don't respond to surveys as a general rule, which probably sounds odd given my work in the industry, but it is an integrity issue.

The first question I ask the hopeful interviewer is which ethics body their company belongs to. Usually the interviewer has no idea, so it stops right there. Ethics bodies like the Association of Market Research Organisations (AMRO) provide a set of guidelines or standards which ensure the integrity of the interviewing company, just like other industries have ethics bodies, such as REINZ for real estate, and the MVDI for motor vehicles. If I'm to provide personal information to a stranger, it's vital that their company is bound by external ethics. Most interviewers cannot supply the information, so we don't get past that point.

If they do name an ethics body, I ask for the phone number of their supervisor, and who the survey is being done for. Ironically, most will claim confidentiality and privacy reasons for not being able to give those details, which raises a red flag.

Door-knocking interviewers must display a photo identification badge that includes their name and a 24-hour 0800 number. This protects both them and you.

Occasionally, I do take part in a survey, but I retain the right to ignore any impertinent or unrealistic question. If the interviewer can't cope with those boundaries, the interview is over; it's important to keep safe from the scumbags out there.

For the 2018 census, due to a temporary lull in my own work, I decided to apply for a census supervisor's job. I tried to fill in the online application form, but it was hopeless; the questions appeared to have been copied from an American template and didn't relate to New Zealand conditions. I did my best and sent it, despite the difficulties and the nonsensical questions. Not surprisingly, given the hopelessness of the application form, the HR company who was advertising the positions apparently had a huge disparity between the number of online 'views' versus those who actually applied. The agency involved had not recruited for census workers before, and I understand from talking to one of their staff members that they were simply overwhelmed by the task. One issue was that they didn't appear to know which towns belonged in certain regions or of the distances involved between regions. For instance, they seemed to think that Blenheim and Tapawera were somehow connected (they are three hours distant by car), yet Brightwater and Richmond (10 minutes) were not.

After applying, I heard nothing from the agency for months, not even a recognition receipt, then out of the blue, I received a phone call for an on-the-spot phone interview. The interviewer seemed to have very little idea of what the job entailed in practical terms or of my region. She had lots of trendy words and phrases, but the substance just wasn't there. I asked her a couple of questions pertaining to the census methodology, such as what the job actually involved, but she had no idea.

Again, I waited to hear, and eventually I received an email saying I had got the job and was to attend a full day's training, but it was for the very next day, in our nearest city, which is one and a half hours' drive away! Less than 24 hours' notice was ridiculous — and impossible. I wonder how many people of supervisor calibre have completely free days just lying around. I phoned the agency and was told that the training day was compulsory or I would lose the job. I withdrew my application. Several days later a representative phoned, and tried very hard to persuade me to reconsider, as they were struggling to find rural supervisors.

By then I had spoken with a couple of experienced interviewers who had applied for census enumerator positions and who were equally frustrated by the process; one of them was a very experienced long-time census worker and even she was finding this new agency very difficult. In light of the fiasco that the 2018 census appeared to become, my withdrawal was an excellent decision.

Sadly, I've developed a very cynical view of one New Zealand government department over the years. It's inevitable that their interviewing staff and I should cross paths out in the field from time to time, but in my experience their lack of professionalism is surprising.

Interviewing in a rural area one afternoon, I noticed two ladies in a department car which was crawling slowly along the road. They appeared to be writing down each emergency services number. Their little low-slung town car was totally unsuitable for the potholed and deeply rutted dirt road, and the driver looked a bit stressed.

I stopped at my next house; these two women parked opposite me. Both had straggly hair and tired eyes, looking like they'd had a rough day. The driver challenged me, pulling her chest high to enforce that they were on 'official government business', recording every dwelling on the road, and if I disturbed people it could make their day more difficult. They were clearly not pleased when I was able to prove that while I worked for a private company, the survey itself was also 'official government business'.

In an attempt to be friendly, I shared that I'd been up through the last gate on the road, which had an emergency services number, but it just identified a forestry skid site. There was no dwelling up there. I also pointed out that where they had just noted one number for a property back down the road a bit, I had been in there and in fact there were four separate dwellings at that site.

These two dishevelled ladies were not inclined to believe me, indicating that they'd ask at the house we were parked beside.

Not to be outsmarted by these frosty women, I hastened to the homeowner's door. The women tottered behind on high heels. One had been silly enough to be wearing a tight skirt, totally unsuitable clothing for rural work! Knocking on the house door, I positioned myself so that the homeowner would see me first. When she answered, I made a bit of a joke of it, saying it was her lucky day to have three of us there at the same time, but I assured her that the others just had a quick question then they'd be on their way. I stepped aside, one of the statistics ladies checked the information I'd given them, and they left, with no thanks or smile for me. Oh well, I tried. However, their car, appearance, lack of accuracy and poor manners certainly inspires little faith in their branch of the department. Having said that, while out working I have met some of their peer interviewers from other regions who have seemed to be very professional and top notch.

20

The human touch

The man on the phone was too depressed to talk, he said. He sounded lost, too tired to care. His voice came in a monotone, with no tension or life. Thoroughly concerned, I asked if he was okay, and he said he would be, eventually. I asked him if he was safe, and he said he had given all his life-threatening stuff to a neighbour to take away.

I asked him if I could phone anyone.

He said no.

I asked him what he was going to do after the phone call, and he said, 'Put my jacket on.'

'Then what?' I asked.

He said, 'Go for a walk along the beach.'

'What will you see?' I asked, desperate to find a way to help him.

'Birds, shitting on rocks,' he said.

Inanely, I said, 'That's nice.'

A strange noise came down the phone. It grew and grew. Belatedly I realised he was laughing, and I started to laugh too. His laughter went on and on. At last, he remembered I was still there.

'Thank you,' he said simply and, with no goodbye, hung up the phone.

I still wonder what his story was and what happened next.

§

Down the phone, I could hear water. Running water. Splashing water. Definitely water. Yet the man being interviewed was clearly in a room of some kind; his answers echoed slightly, as though he was in a large, almost empty space. He was unhurried, giving thoughtful consideration to each question response. The interview time had been selected by him when I made contact a few days earlier.

At the end of the interview, I could no longer contain my curiosity. Breaking the rules about privacy, I asked him, very politely, 'Where are you?'

He laughed, then admitted, slightly sheepishly, that the entire interview had been conducted while he lazed in his bath, with a glass of wine in hand and a wonderful view down his valley through his hilltop home's floor-to-ceiling windows. Quite simply, he was in his happy place.

I was just grateful that we do not do video calls.

The elderly lady had just arrived home as I turned into her driveway. Normally, I would pass her by, giving her time to get organised before I returned, but this lady was clearly struggling, quite out of breath, and the groceries looked way too heavy for her. I offered to give her a hand, one human to another. She sat on a chair by her door and watched while I took her groceries from her car, to her door, where I placed them on the mat. She asked me to take them inside for her, but I was very aware of not being seen to be taking advantage, so first I explained who I was and that I was conducting interviews in the area on behalf of the local council about things like water, roads and footpaths. I also commented that it would be fine for me to come back another day to interview her. She seemed happy and insisted quite firmly that I take in her groceries, and 'finish the job'.

Once inside, this lovely lady, still bent over and puffing at a level I found concerning, asked if I would mind making her a cup of tea as she wasn't feeling great. She certainly didn't look great, so I agreed and sounded her out about whether she had support or a St John alarm. This required some tact, as it's way outside my interviewer role to do such a thing, but I was genuinely concerned for her welfare.

Between breaths she assured me she had an alarm and was not afraid to use it. She then proudly showed me photos of her family, grandchildren, deceased husband and others. I was certain at this point that I would not be interviewing her today, as she looked very tired. She asked me to put her purse in the drawer where she kept her financial stuff, which left me more than a little uncomfortable. I do not like being privy to other people's security.

Once she was looking more stable, and I had locked her car for her, I made my goodbyes, saying I would come back another day when she was likely to be a bit better.

'No,' she said very firmly. 'I won't be taking part. It would be a breach of my privacy. What I think about the roads is none of your business. However, thank you so much for helping me. You were very kind.'

And with that, she shut the door, leaving me slightly taken aback on the doorstep.

Approaching a home once, I heard the unmistakable sounds of a person working on a car in the open garage. My enquiring call was answered with an 'In here' from a young man who was covered in oil and grease. From under the car bonnet, he turned his head to look at me, and I hastily explained what I was doing.

'Here, hold this,' he said, handing me a wrench. 'How long will the interview take?'

When I said just a quarter of an hour max, he grunted, and carried on working. The minutes crawled by, with me still holding the wrench. The young man occasionally swore at the car, mentioning its dubious parentage, and any attempt by me at conversation or starting the interview was just met with more grunts.

At last he straightened up, took the wrench from me, and said, 'Righto, let's do this thing.'

After the interview, he made an odd comment about how right it was that we'd taken up exactly the same amount of each other's time. I queried it, at which point he admitted that holding the wrench had been just a ploy. He had decided that if I wanted 15 minutes of his time, he was entitled to 15 minutes of mine first, whether it was useful to him or not!

What he didn't know was that his was the last interview of a very big job. Exhausted, and having just spent two hours fruitlessly looking for someone of his age and gender, I would have held that wrench for an hour if it meant I got to interview him.

I like to think that I'm not superstitious, but why did the folk living at number 666 have a black cat? For another survey I was interviewing by phone, getting feedback from businesses who had got registration in the previous year. All was well, until interview number 13; a wee shiver went up my spine when it turned out to be a firm of funeral directors. The sensible side of me laughs, but there's always that little voice at my shoulder sounding a warning.

Another day where all warning bells went off happened entirely unexpectedly. The tidy cottage I approached clearly belonged to an older person. Even if the long witches-britches-style underwear hanging on the clothesline didn't say it, the motorised scooter and cute sign saying 'Grandma's house' certainly did. The cottage's back door was wide open, the TV was blaring and something was cooking on the stove. Yet there was no reply to my knock. I tried again. Meanwhile the stuff on the stove was sending out burning smells. I called out. No reply. This is when it gets tricky. Where was this grandma? Should I enter the home of a stranger to save the burning food? It occurred to me that I was in trouble either way but, realistically, I couldn't just stand there and watch her lunch burn. My imagination was running wild . . . would the lunch eventually catch fire and burn her house down? If I stepped inside, was I breaking the law? I could see the headlines: 'Interviewer caught intruding' or, worse, 'Interviewer watched house burn to the ground'. What to do?

Looking for a compromise, and without stepping foot into her home, I reached into her kitchen as far as I could, but my arms just weren't long enough to get to that pot on the stove. Frustrated, and still hoping the homeowner would turn up, I looked around for something to help. Spotting a walking stick on the mobility scooter, I grabbed the stick and, holding it by the foot end, poked the handle around the pot. Holding my breath, I gently pulled, desperate not to tip the whole lot onto the floor. Imagine if the lady returned to find her lunch upended! Concentrating hard, I managed to shift the pot off the element to safety. I couldn't do anything about the element itself, so had to just hope that the lady would notice the still-hot element and not burn herself.

Next was the original problem: where was the homeowner? Assuming she was elderly, could she be lying on the floor somewhere, hurt or ill? I already knew that there was no one home at the house next door, so I couldn't ask a neighbour for advice. If this lady needed help, it was likely to be an emergency. Did that give me the right to enter her home? What to do? I went around the outside of the cottage, peering cautiously into each window, which would have looked dodgy to any passer-by, had there been any. If the lady was in another room, I didn't want to scare seven bells out of her by looking like a peeping Tom! Any minute now I would hear the wail of police sirens. If she was on the floor, would I even see her? Maybe a leg, a pool of blood, a knocked-over lamp?

Having looked in every window I could (the toilet window was too high), and relieved to not spot anything odd, it still left the questions: where was she and was she okay? I had been calling out every few minutes, and getting no response, yet she had to be nearby. No one goes far leaving their lunch and TV on, and the mobility scooter parked at the door suggested a short walk at most.

Failing any luck, and running out of ideas, I decided to check the outbuildings — and that's when I found her, asleep in the glasshouse! At first, I thought she was dead, she looked so peaceful. I called gently, and she woke up with a start. Once we got the explanations out of the way, we both had a chuckle, and all was well. She had gone to her glasshouse to get some herbs to add to her lunch but, feeling tired, sat down for a moment in her favourite chair. It was so comfortable that, combined with the warmth of the glasshouse and the garden's peacefulness, she had simply dozed off. She was very grateful that I had saved her lunch.

21
Away from home

Sometimes it feels like it's going to be a long day, even before I set out from home. In the middle of a cold snap, I was anticipating frosty or icy roads, particularly over a mountain range which sits between me and the remote area I was heading to. Setting out early meant very little traffic, and once I got climbing, I was pleased to be in a four-wheel-drive, with its lovely grippy tyres, warm heater and radio tuned to my favourite station. I had packed a thermos, and winter gear like gloves, in case I got stuck anywhere. Rounding a corner near the top, I came across a young family who had skidded off the road, into the scrub. Their car, an older-model medium-sized Corolla, was unharmed, as were they, but it was obvious that they weren't going anywhere by themselves. Fortunately, my four-wheel-drive has a winch on the front, so I wrapped up warm and offered a hand. The family were freezing cold, so my thermos was quickly used to warm cold bellies, while I set up ready to pull them out. By the time I had attached the winch under their car, which could only be done by lying on the snow, the cold was creeping through my layers, so I was pleased to get the family's car out fairly quickly. Even with gloves, my hands were growing numb, and I realised that it would be a while before warmth seeped back in, even with the heater on full. I then followed the family down to the bottom, way behind my planned time schedule. At the next village, I stopped to get a hot drink and was dismayed to find that some of my clothes were filthy; it wasn't just the cold that had found its way through my layers.

So it was that I found myself purchasing a pair of socks, a pair of black jeans, and a new jersey, before I could even knock on the first door. There's nothing like having spent your earnings before you even get there!

Sometimes, driving home after a long day of meeting and interviewing strangers, I find myself driving on autopilot, or worse, nearly falling asleep, and it's time to take a short break. Ten-minute naps work quite well, but the issue is, where? As a woman on my own, and heading home with lots of people's personal details in my files, security is a real issue. Instinct says to find somewhere dark and silent, out of sight, where I can lock the doors, turn off the headlights, and become invisible. The problem with that is if an issue arises, like someone with crime on their mind noticing me, I would be totally vulnerable, with no one around to see or prevent what might happen.

The alternative is to park out in the open, near light, but then I feel like a rabbit in headlights, exposed and an easy target. The answer is simpler: I try to find a truck park-up spot, where truckies are also taking a break. I slip my car in between their trucks, hoping that there's safety in numbers. They probably don't notice me, but the good news is that if they've thought it odd, they've had the manners not to comment!

Occasionally, a survey requires motel stays, especially if it involves working in a different or remote region. Friends comment that I'm lucky and that it sounds wonderful; a night to eat whatever I like at a restaurant and then have an evening all to myself. The motels are always clean, warm and sterile. However, they usually only offer the free-to-air channels on the TV, and anything I take to pass the time has to be lugged in from the car. To get the most out of the interviewing time, it's normal to work until nearly dark (and sometimes later if folk have made an appointment), so there's no enjoying the sights of the village or going for walks on the beach. While it's nice to read a book or watch a TV programme uninterrupted, the reality is that eating out alone, and spending a night away from home with no fun attached, is not my idea of a treat. There's also no opportunity to wind down with a 'how was your day?' chat, or conversation about other topics to take my mind off the work. Usually, I just find food, check my paperwork, watch a programme and read to sleep . . . nothing exciting or romantic at all!

22
Outside the norm

The 1970s HardiePlank house at the end of a long drive should have been quite forgettable, sitting in a subdivision of similar houses all packed in together on little squares of grass hemmed by timber fencing. The house was a rectangular box, totally unremarkable, with a garage door that had given up, and any colour on the exterior walls long since sucked off, leaving a pale grey undercoat. Every window framed a plethora of soft toys and window ornaments, but, given that there was no exterior view worth looking at, I was not that surprised. Folk often adorn their windows if there is no expansive view to admire. Kids' bikes were strewn about the garage forecourt, old netball hoops on tall poles leaned at impossible angles, a trampoline had a mat which was barely hanging on, and a swimming pool lounged across a corner, full of toys but no water. A couple of shrubs bravely clung to life partway along the fence line, and against all odds, one had a blush of pink flowers poking through the branches. In the driveway was a bright red sporty-type car, looking very new and totally out of place.

Getting to the recessed back door was a bit tricky, with shoes of every size and shape fighting for space, along with boots, raincoats and school bags. Looking at the footwear, it was impossible to guess the ages or genders of who might live in the house, as there appeared to be every size from toddler to teenager, along with adult. I tried pressing what had once been the doorbell, but nothing resounded within, so I knocked.

A lovely bright energetic woman in her late thirties answered the door, dressed in smart jeans and with a figure straight out of trendy magazines. She invited me in, gaily apologising for the mess, and led me to the kitchen. Mess? There was stuff everywhere! New stuff, old stuff, food leftovers on plates, half-drunk drinks with mould across the top, clothes in various stages of being washed or dried, and so much junk. Each wall had stuff piled high against it, and a wall unit groaned under the weight of boxes, books, knick-knacks. Any 'spare' wall space was covered in kids' art, dated and named. Every chair was littered with anything from laptops to boxes of heaven-knows-what, and there was just enough space to walk from room to room. It took me a few minutes to even spot the child watching preschool TV. The child was one of three, as it turned out, and all were open-faced, happy, confident kids. One tried to show me his telescope, and another wanted to read me a book which was far more advanced than I would have expected for the age. The mum was keen to be interviewed, though her cell phone kept on interrupting, as she answered every message immediately. Her answers to the interview were very on point.

She invited me to have a cuppa with her and, against my normal practice, I agreed. There was something about this woman that was very appealing, making you want to spend time with her. During the cuppa, she offered some insight into all the stuff. She said she loved shopping; the bargain was like a drug. She bought stuff for the high it gave her, and then gave most of it away. Occasionally, she would have a garage sale or donate a pile to the op-shop. She said it was a better vice than gambling or smoking, and she had no guilt at all. She also commented about the housework, saying that she simply didn't care. As long as everyone was healthy, housework was overrated and a complete waste of time. The thing that really stuck was how little importance she placed on conforming to social expectations, achieving her goals and happiness in her own way.

Sometimes folk's perfectly legal activities can prove a real problem. I don't smoke. I did in my younger days, but not now. With asthmatic tendencies, smoke can cause coughing fits, which is never a good look for an interviewer, but there's always the unwelcome worry of passive smoking. Sitting in someone's home, where the windows are invariably shut, with a heavy cloud of smoke creating a haze in the room, really challenges me. I imagine cancer sneaking in with glorious celebration, catching another victim.

Sometimes I will find a way to suggest that we do the interview outside, if I am worried about the smoke, but usually the person is averse to the idea, so I have to suffer the lack of fresh air, the smells and the fear. Cancer should not be considered a reasonable consequence of working as an interviewer, yet I have not been able to come up with a truly satisfactory solution which won't cause offence to the person whose views are entitled to be included in the results.

Similarly, a room full of folk drinking can be an interesting challenge, as their inhibitions are lowered while their opinions are heightened. I will not interview someone who is drunk, and I draw the line at entering anywhere that smells of marijuana. Some folk try to hide what they are doing, forgetting that the smell hangs around, while others are quite blatant and really don't care. One guy I interviewed in a rural area was tending the plants in his glasshouse while I interviewed him. As a gardener I am always keen to see what other gardeners are doing, and have gathered many ideas along the way, but what this gardener propagated among his vegetables would never be seen in my glasshouse! It was a very healthy crop, though, lush, well-fed and pretty to look at.

Other law breakers make me really have to sit on my emotions. On a beautiful spring day, I was interviewing in an estate that had large comfortable homes overlooking acres of shared olive grove. Each home was privately owned, along with a couple of acres, but the residents pooled resources so that they all got an income from their olives. The estate had no fences, and the style of houses meant that the area had a Tuscany feel to it. At each house the people were just lovely, welcoming and understanding of the work I was doing.

That is, until the very last house in the whole estate. Their tree-lined driveway opened into a large courtyard area, with stunning views out to sea, and a deep-oak welcome sign hung across the entranceway. Everything was immaculately presented, complete with a friendly overweight black Labrador who waddled over to greet me. I was completely lulled, partly because the whole neighbourhood had been a rewarding and welcoming place to work.

A four-wheel-drive vehicle was parked facing outwards on the drive, with a large recreational boat attached which was clearly being loaded for a fishing trip. As I was there to interview about fishing, it seemed fortuitous.

I was in for a rude awakening.

The 'gentleman' who approached me asked quite brusquely what I was there for, and once I told him that the survey was about recreational fishing, he went right off. The gist of it was that no one was going to tell him where to fish or what size he could catch and the law was an ass. He really went to town with his right to do whatever he wanted. I tried hard, with a warmth I was definitely not feeling, to get him to understand that if he'd do the interview, he would be helping to improve things for recreational fishers, but he wasn't having a bar of it. Apparently, the current fishing laws didn't apply to him, and he wasn't going to assist those bureaucratic idiots in Wellington to make any new ones. He was extraordinarily abusive and very clear that he fished wherever he liked, including in marine reserves, and he hadn't been caught so it didn't matter.

As a fisher myself, and a supporter of protecting our fish reserves so that everyone can have a good day fishing, I was boiling inside at his sheer arrogance, but of course the smile stayed pinned to my face and the professionalism blocked any personal reaction.

As he was pontificating to me, the man was loading his boat with supplies. Unbelievably, there were six large boxes of beer going in, for a half day's fishing. He was taking his two teenage boys and wife out and they were going to have a good time. At least a picnic hamper went in too. The life jackets got left in the garage because, as he explained to his wife when she queried it, they were only going out into the bay. I was astonished that someone of his income level did not have the intelligence to realise how many rules he was breaking, and the risks he was taking, for his fun.

As I turned away, I noticed that the boat trailer registration had expired; the temptation to dob the man in to the police was oh so strong. I didn't, of course, but it's hard not to feel like taking a tiny bit of revenge when I've been abused by someone who thinks himself above the law like he did.

§

I'm very good at getting myself into a pickle at the front door, even before locating the person I need to interview!

Hearing a lot of banging going on through the open door of the garage beside the house I was approaching, and seeing a gent working on an engineering project of some kind, I headed directly for him, rather than going around the back of the house to find the main entrance. Spotting me, the man waved his hand in the air, indicating the house, and said, 'Go see her indoors. She'll help you.' I hadn't even opened my mouth at this stage, so he had no idea who I was or what I wanted. Thanking him, I carried on to the house. The lady was lovely, and would have been a pleasure to interview, but it soon became clear that the criteria for the survey meant that it was the husband that I had to talk to. It's a bit tricky going back to someone who has already decided that you should be talking to someone else. Are they truly busy or just against surveys? I try to make light of it, slightly apologetic but also with a touch of humour about Murphy's law, in the hope that he will see it the same way.

In this case, the man had a response I'd not met before. 'What's this?' he asked, pointing to a Crescent spanner. I replied, slightly puzzled. He gave a grunt. Next it was an 'Andy' shovel he asked me to identify. Then a hacksaw. I still wasn't entirely sure what was going on, but I played along. He got me to identify about a dozen items, even throwing in a curve ball by asking what a couple of the items were for. Each time I answered, he would just give a grunt. I wondered what my boss would think if she could hear all this.

At last, I was able to bring the test to an end and introduce the survey itself. He readily agreed to be interviewed, and at his suggestion we retired to their beautiful garden, to sit among lovely flowering borders and under a sun umbrella, and got it done. As I was saying my goodbyes and thanks, he said, with a twinkle in his eye, 'I only did it because you knew something about my workshop; I've got no truck with those bloody townies that come in here and have no idea. Useless they are. Don't deserve a man's time.'

Similarly, at another home workshop, a gent told me after the interview that he'd only done it as I'd not flinched at shaking his grease-covered paws!

Communities can have an interesting mix of folk. Trudging up what should have been a road but was more like a piece of runway tarmac thrown carelessly over a strip of hill, I couldn't help but feel that the owners of the closely packed two-bedroom houses lining the street had either misunderstood or rejected that big word: maintenance. Even the local sparrows had not bothered with a tidy appearance, hopping about a broken rubbish bin in a ruffled kind of way.

The road's surface had broken edges, especially where vehicles had crossed into areas euphemistically called driveways. The green areas around each home could not be called lawn or garden, however optimistically viewed, though a lemon tree out the front of one house looked like a Christmas tree, adorned with a mass of ripe fruit. You need resilience to thrive on this, the shady side of the hill.

I knocked on the door of the third house, as dictated by our randomising factor, and a 60-plus woman on crutches came out. She had tripped on the 'road' and broken her leg. Now she was housebound, as the steepness and surface of the road prevented her using the crutches safely.

The third home from the crutches lady housed a very friendly young family. They had a double income but despite working alongside budget advice were still dependent on a food bank to feed their children the treats in life like apples and vegetables. With no car or public transport, they walked everywhere, so they could only buy what they could carry, while still pushing the child buggy and holding their other child's hand.

Making my way back down the hill, visiting homes on the other side of the road, I came across a weatherboard house which had probably once been painted a darkish yellow colour, but it was hard to tell, under the black sooty mould and overgrown ivy. Out the back, under an old carport, I discovered five men in various stages of disrepair, surrounded by stacks and stacks of empty beer bottles. They clearly had on some kind of uniform: holey jeans, old boots, ripped jerseys and beanies, housing skinny frames and growing a mandatory beard and straggly hair. The men gaily invited me to join their committee meeting, which I regretfully declined, citing the 'no alcohol' rule. Having worked out who it was I needed to interview, I offered to make an appointment, or move away so that his responses could be private, but he would have none of it. Apparently, they were all about 'total honesty' — no secrets here. So, I interviewed the gent from where I stood, having politely declined to join him on the couch, among guffaws from the others. They seemed a friendly, if filthy, bunch, and I needed to match the friendliness but not the dirt, in a professional way.

When we were almost through the interview, the gent asked after one of my adult children, by name. I was totally startled and responded in a vague kind of way. He then told his mates all about the valley I live in and related a wee story from years before. I listened, puzzled as to how he knew those things. It wasn't until the end of the interview, when I asked for his name for the paperwork, that the mystery was solved, but the answer left me gobsmacked. The last time I had seen this man, he was a successful businessman, with a home, family and smart car, and he had been very active in his community. It was difficult to reconcile the memory with the image in front of me. He must have sensed my confusion, as he said, 'Drink my dear, drink,' and with that, he turned to his mates, proposed a toast to alcoholism, and they all joined in, laughing. They were still laughing when I left to find my next interview.

One of the few times that I felt genuinely afraid for my well-being was on a blustery day when I was working in an area which was made up of lifestyle-type blocks spread out over clay hills, with pine trees scattered across brown windswept paddocks. I was following a private road, and every few minutes another group of buildings and a home of some description would appear. There were house buses, cabins, at least two mansions with stunning sea views, and several other homes. Most had a variety of sheds, yards and animals in the outlying parts of the properties. The road itself was quite rough, and I was thankful for the four-wheel-drive abilities of my car; it's reassuring to know the capabilitiy is there.

As I approached one house, I was surprised to see it was stucco, meaning it had probably been built in the 1960s, as most of the blocks had looked quite new. I discovered later that this was the original farmhouse, and that the private road had another end to it, so this property was not, in fact, far from a sealed road.

A couple of large dogs came rushing out and had a sniff around. Someone called them back, and they retreated to lie on the lawn, watching in a relaxed manner. A lady who looked to be in her seventies, but was probably 20 years younger, came to the veranda, wiping her hands on her apron, and called out, 'Watcha want?' I walked over to be nearer her, so as not to shout, and explained what I was doing. She said I had better come in. Following her inside, I got a strong impression of a hunting and mechanically-minded family, as there was hunting gear, camouflage-type clothing, motorbike and car parts, and oily clothes strewn around. The kitchen was incredibly dirty, with food packets, smokes, beer cans and paraphernalia spread across benches, and the smell of dog was very strong. The interior of the house was a dirty green/grey colour, and clearly hadn't seen a cloth or paintbrush for a long time. Whatever was cooking on the stove, in an enormous urn, was a grey gurgling mess, yet seemed to have no smell.

I began to interview the woman, while she was stirring the pot. She seemed okay, if unkempt and possibly not having been in a shower for a while. Her brownish hair was very dull and looked like it was trying to roll into dreadlocks. What struck me though was her eyes; they were dull, as if life was simply too big and she had meekly submitted. She answered everything in a monotone and seemed to lack emotion. She certainly failed to express an opinion on anything.

About halfway through the interview, a group of blokes appeared, arriving loudly and quite aggressively. They seemed to be four brothers, her sons, all in their late twenties and early thirties. They demanded to know not only what I was doing there but, more worryingly, had I been poking my nose into the sheds and farm buildings on the place? One put his face close to mine and said,

'There'll be trouble if she's been near our sheds.' The mother practically begged them to accept that I hadn't seen anything. Her fear was quite palpable. Another insisted on seeing everything I'd written down, which was awkward as it was their mother's right to privacy, but she quickly assured me it was fine. He made her change one of her answers. One of the others disappeared from the room, then returned a couple of minutes later with a rifle, which he proceeded to wipe with a cloth as though cleaning it, all the while looking at me and asking his mother if she was sure that I hadn't been prying around the sheds.

I was terrified, absolutely terrified. These guys were menacing, and clearly had total control over their mother. In an effort to keep things normal, I continued with the interview, but I just wanted to run. I was so outnumbered, and it felt as though one wrong move from me and they would pounce. After the interview, two of the men escorted me back to my car, all but carrying me by the elbows they were walking so close. I have no idea what they were hiding in their sheds, and don't want to know, but I really felt for their mother.

At the next house I went to, having taken a very deep breath, the lovely man I interviewed said to me, as I was leaving, 'If I was you, I wouldn't call at the stucco house. They're a weird lot up there.' Don't I know it.

23
Recognition

Stopping at a village store to grab some much-needed lunch one Sunday, I was accosted by a gent who very rudely insisted that I get some mustard down from the top shelf for him. The language he used was certainly not fit for church, and his tone suggested he'd just got an oversized tax bill. There was no thank you when I did as he asked, and he stomped off. Two aisles later and he was waiting for me. The f*@*^*@ toothpaste he wanted was out of reach. Not wishing to cause a scene, again I complied. Then I quickly retreated, found what I wanted for my lunch, and went to the checkout. Unfortunately, he got there just after I did, and berated me for not being willing to let an old man go first. I was mortified and stepped aside. Through he went, without another glance at me. It was then the poor checkout woman's turn for a tirade. She appeared to have come across him before, as she didn't turn a hair at either his language or criticism; I admired her calm and ability to just carry on as though he was wishing her a good day. He took forever, checking every price was correct, and that the dates were fine on the products. That checkout lady was a saint and deserved a medal. At last, this rude man was done. I'm pretty sure I wasn't the only person who was relieved to see him go. There are some folk you just don't want to come across ever again.

Later that day, I knocked on the door of a pleasant-looking suburban house, and who should come to the door but the elderly gent from the store. Not being able to run, I did my usual introduction, fully expecting to be told to get lost. Not only did he readily agree to the interview but he gave no sign of recognition, and what's more, he was totally pleasant and courteous throughout. Not a swear word or grump in sight. If he hadn't been wearing the same clothes, I would have been convinced that he had a twin brother — a grumpy, rude, obnoxious twin brother.

Most interviews are completed quickly, with a brief connection simply recording a person's opinions or what they engage in. By the time I get home, having completed several interviews in the day, there are only impressions left, unless someone or something has stood out. Names, individual details and addresses are long gone.

This can have an interesting after-affect. I've had folk approach me in public, when I've not been working, and start chatting to me as though I should know them. It's too embarrassing to admit that they are only vaguely familiar, but the bigger danger is if I do remember them as I have to be very careful to take their lead and not disclose, in front of their companions, anything they may have said or done during the interview.

One weekend, I was attending a horse show, enjoying the atmosphere, the sun and my children's involvement with their ponies. Interviewing was well out of the picture, with no current surveys under way, and I was having a well-earned break. A lady who I'd interviewed a few weeks before suddenly appeared right in my face. She is taller than me and quite formidably built. The sun disappeared behind her frame, leaving me in full shadow.

She sailed into me, long and loud, giving me her opinion about the topics that the survey had been about. She had obviously been giving it some thought, and now she really wanted to have her say, in full. My daughter was in the ring competing and I was supposed to be watching, providing much-needed mother support, but this woman was having none of it. She went on and on, so loudly that other people were clearly enjoying eavesdropping. I tried to manoeuvre myself to get a view of my daughter, and in the end the only place I could achieve it was by peering underneath this woman's very floppy armpit. Suddenly she demanded, 'Why are you looking at my boob?' Flustered, I mumbled something about my daughter, hoping to get a break, but she was undeterred and carried on. The opinions she was expecting me to agree with don't match my own, but due to the need for discretion and privacy as an interviewer I cannot disagree or correct a respondent. Eventually, she went off, completely satisfied that she'd had her say. Sadly, I had missed most of my daughter's performance but was saved from any ruinous confession when it was announced that she had won her class. Fortunately, my daughter came out of the ring so ecstatic that she didn't notice that I had no feedback for her.

When being introduced to someone at a social event, it's not uncommon for the person to study me closely, clearly puzzling over the feeling that they've met me before, but not quite able to put their finger on it. There follows a hilarious verbal dance where they try to work out the connection, by asking what school I went to, where have I worked, what sports I've been involved with. For them, the mystery deepens, but of course I cannot let them off the hook by reminding them that I've interviewed them, as doing so could jeopardise their confidentiality.

24
After the survey

One of the privileges of working in non-commercial interviewing is that the interviewer can usually find the results of any survey in the public arena, a few months later. In my local area, it's not unusual to see the district council release the results to media, though sometimes I am surprised at the outcomes, as the impression I had got from the interviews is a bit different from the overall result. This happened over a local proposal that I personally lobbied against. During the interviewing period I had been a bit startled and disappointed that none of the respondents I interviewed had raised the topic; clearly, they had different priorities to me. While this showed that I was being truly impartial, I was frustrated on a personal level that no one seemed to care enough to mention the issue. I was the only local interviewer on this job, with a significant number of out-of-district interviewers also undertaking the resident contacts. Imagine my surprise then when I saw the results, to find that a significant number of respondents had indeed raised the issue. It appears that I had simply struck a sample which had a slight anomaly, yet again proving why all surveys need to make sure that the number of interviews done irons out any skews.

Over the years, I have been involved in surveys being conducted for the World Health Organisation, Organisation for Economic Co-operation and Development and others. When they undertake these international studies, across several countries at the same time, it gives me a good feeling to know that I am a tiny part of a huge operation that is designed to help folk worldwide. When the results come out, it can be interesting to read the findings and analysis. One of these is the skills study of the adult population which can be found on the OECD website.

At least 20 per cent of all interviews are audited, usually via a phone call by a supervisor to a respondent. This is to ensure that the interviewer is working correctly, accurately and leaving a good impression. Sometimes the respondent has no recollection of being interviewed, which can be a little daunting as it raises the question of whether an interview really did take place there, or whether the interviewer sat in their car and made it up. If they had made it up, how did they get the person's name and correct phone number? Usually, a little prompting brings about the respondent's recall. The audit checks that the correct person was interviewed, how long it took and whether there were any issues. Sometimes the respondent wants to change an answer or expand on what they said in the original interview, not understanding that the time is past for that. One of the hardest things to audit is how long the interview took.

For the person who enjoyed the experience, time flew by so they will genuinely believe that it took a much shorter time than it did. Conversely, the person who found the interview invasive will think it took much longer. Then there's the subjective topic of what is too long. I called a lady who said the interview took forever and shouldn't be allowed. When pressed for the actual length, she said it was at least five minutes — far too long! It would have taken about 10 minutes, but nevertheless, she was resolutely certain in what she believed, and I wasn't going to correct her.

Auditing has another pitfall: how to address the person. In the original interview, the person isn't normally asked for their name until the end, by which time a rapport is established and the respondent is feeling reassured by the content of the interview. As it's not usual to ask for surnames, in order to maintain privacy, the respondent will be listed as 'George', 'Mary' etc.

However, as the area manager, when I phone to audit the interview and address the respondent as 'George' or 'Mary', many, particularly the elderly, get a little offended. I am a stranger, so it's rude to address them by their first name. I always apologise if I sense a negative reaction and remind them that they were not asked for their surname. Generally, they accept that, but it can be tricky.

Occasionally when auditing a new interviewer, I will resort to Google maps to ensure that they did indeed go to the designated houses rather than picking the easy or friendly-looking homes. This is a useful tool and has on two occasions led me to then take a drive to check it out more fully. In one case the interviewer had done everything correctly, and in the other, the interviewer had not recognised a driveway in a rural area as being just that. When I got there, I could understand it, as there was no letterbox and just a rutted track which disappeared over a rise, giving little hint of the dwelling further on.

This reminded me of a rural property I went to which had one letterbox and a house clearly visible from the road. I did an interview in the home, and the resident was thoroughly engaged in the topic. As I was about to leave, he asked if I was going to interview at the other homes on the same property. 'What homes?' I asked. It transpired that there were a further five homes on the rural site, plus two house buses, all secreted away in bush areas well out of view and all completely illegal, with no building consents. It was important to the residents that there be no visible sign of their homes, hence just the one letterbox. I interviewed in a couple of the homes, and they were beautiful, with a mix of handcrafted timber and recycled materials, creating a warm and cosy atmosphere. They were off-grid and had extensive fruit and vegetable plots. There were several happy, relaxed children running around. The respondents were clearly well-educated and very thoughtful in their responses to the survey's questions. I did ask one inhabitant how the houses had come about, and she said the residents were all from the same family. None of them could afford a home, so they had pooled their resources. The little community had evolved over time, and they had no intention of ever bothering with the expenses of consents and the like; their focus was entirely on raising their children to be healthy, educated and socially aware members of the world, resilient and grounded. I left there wondering how the building consent/resource consent process would have impacted on their goals and outcomes, and at what expense. It was a privilege to have been trusted with their vulnerability.

25
Other interviewers' stories

Mostly interviewers work alone, and if there is a problem or a tale to tell, they are confined to sharing with their supervisor. As an area supervisor, overseeing up to eight interviewers, and covering an area of around 25,000 square kilometres, I get to hear snippets of experiences that are similar to my own. However, there are a couple of stories which I have heard from further afield which have given me pause for thought.

The first is from a census worker, who was going door to door delivering census forms. She was invited into a home which had a lot of firearms on display. While unusual, this did not rattle her; it was the live grenade on the table which absorbed all of her attention!

In another incident, an interviewer was driving home from a two-day trip to a remote area. She was exhausted, and was looking forward to her own warm bath, her own bed and a relaxing evening. Suddenly, her car felt heavy to steer on a right-hand bend and grimly she realised that she had a flat tyre. This woman was very capable, and a flat tyre would normally just be a nuisance, but she was already running on low, and this was the last straw. She got everything out, ready to change the tyre, but she had little strength left to get the wheel nuts undone. The area she was stranded in was reasonably remote, so there was little traffic. She struggled and fought with the nuts, but they weren't budging. Almost in tears, she imagined herself marooned for the night, with only a bag of apples to eat and hardly any water left. What's more, it looked like it was going to be very cold, and she was certainly not prepared for that. It just couldn't get any worse.

Then, a small group of motorcycle gang members came around the corner. She viewed their approach with dismay; with no cell-phone coverage and no other traffic, she was totally vulnerable. The tattooed, black-leather-adorned hairy figures pulled over and approached her. She was terrified, tired and helpless. It didn't help that some of the tattoos had quite aggressive words, like 'hate' and 'revenge'.

One of the men took the wrench from her hand and proceeded to change the tyre. The others stood around talking and laughing, discussing their bikes and the road with each other. She could not believe the kindness of these strangers and felt ashamed that she had judged them by their looks. She offered them her bag of apples, which they gladly accepted, and she found herself sitting on the side of the road with a bunch of patched motorcycle gang members, munching on an apple and listening to their stories.

Driving home afterwards, she found herself singing;

the encounter had truly lifted her day.

One of the phone surveys that I was involved in was following up with mothers of newborn babies. Most of these women had cell phones only, so we had no idea which part of the country we were phoning into. In my calling I came across a delightful cross-section of mums from all walks of life, and they all seemed to have two things in common: tiredness from lack of sleep and a love of talking about their baby! I thoroughly enjoyed the contacts and had a high response rate. Not all interviewers had it so good, though. One of my peers phoned a young mother, and when she explained what she was calling about, the mum burst into tears; the baby had died of cot death the week before. The poor interviewer. She felt her call had been unwittingly very cruel, and it left her badly shaken. There was nothing she could do to make this situation any better, and I really felt for her.

26
The happiest man alive

On a gravel road, tucked into the bush in a secluded valley, I came across a little two-room cottage from a bygone era. Smoke was puffing out of the chimney at one end while two sash windows faced the road, underneath an iron roof. I went around the cottage to find the back door and was met by a lovely old hunting dog, which had clearly had his last days running the hills.

Down a concrete path I could see a little shed which held a long-drop, and outside was a concrete laundry tub with a single tap. A shirt and a pair of socks flapped on the fence. There was a comprehensive vegetable patch, with a great range of very healthy-looking plants.

A concrete step led up to the cottage's wooden door and from inside, an elderly man's voice invited me in. There was sacking on the walls, a coal range, a Formica table with two chairs and a couple of very old lounge chairs. Through an internal door I could see a bed strewn with old blankets, in a dark room.

The old man didn't rise from his chair but told me to sit opposite. He was puffing away on a pipe, and his fingers had the yellow stain of tobacco. His very holey singlet revealed sun-browned hardened skin, and he had elderly muscles which could probably still outwork most folk.

Contrary to his appearance, and that of his home, this man turned out to be well-travelled and well-read. He didn't bother with television, internet or smartphones, saying his network of good friends and the library were more than enough. He proudly showed me a photo of his daughter who was 'something big in the city'.

He also stated quite matter-of-factly that he had saved enough money, while he was in the workforce, to live as comfortably as he wanted, so each month he donated all of his superannuation to charity. But the reason that he stands out in my memory completely overrides his living and financial situation. This man, living with his dog in a battered old cottage, looking out onto the hills, and smoking his pipe, patted his dog and told me that he was the happiest man alive.

About the author

TRISH PALMER has had the privilege of interviewing folk in their own homes for over 25 years, either door to door or over the phone. She also farms in a quiet rural valley, off-grid, where she is blessed with the essentials in life: family, friends, fun and food. As well as coastal fishing, she enjoys gold panning, reading, exploring, and playing games like Dominion and Catan. Laughter, respect and living lightly on this planet underline most of her philosophies. Local issues often provoke her to action, and she can't bear inequitable practices.

Trish's fiction work has been published in short story anthologies and nominated for the odd award or two, which she finds satisfying. Several plays have been selected for production, including in Europe. Her poetry has survived live poets' evenings, with kind audience feedback.

Trish writes with pen and paper. Editing happens only when the work is transferred to the computer, and each story has to survive being read to a couple of special folk before it is allowed out in public. She likes to lighten the reader's day through laughter, or by being thought-provoking, so her work tends to be humorous or it tackles social issues, and often both. Her time interviewing people in a wide range of situations has exposed her to many of the realities of life in New Zealand, and this has impacted on her writing.

    Whether working on the farm, restoring the native bush block or tending the organic garden, her stories pop up and insist on being written. Sometimes they make her laugh out loud when they arrive, which can be a bit disconcerting to anyone nearby. Since some people find such things important, Trish should mention that she has a Diploma in Creative Writing and is involved with the local branch of the New Zealand Society of Authors, enjoying sharing her writing journey with fellow authors.